CHRISTIANITY
AND
AMERICAN FREEMASONRY

CHRISTIANITY
AND
AMERICAN FREEMASONRY

William J. Whalen

THIRD EDITION

IGNATIUS PRESS   SAN FRANCISCO

CONTENTS

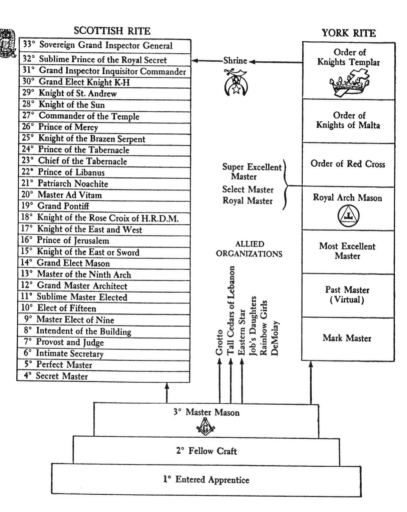

SCOTTISH RITE	ALLIED ORGANIZATIONS	YORK RITE

SCOTTISH RITE

| 33° Sovereign Grand Inspector General |
| 32° Sublime Prince of the Royal Secret |
| 31° Grand Inspector Inquisitor Commander |
| 30° Grand Elect Knight K-H |
| 29° Knight of St. Andrew |
| 28° Knight of the Sun |
| 27° Commander of the Temple |
| 26° Prince of Mercy |
| 25° Knight of the Brazen Serpent |
| 24° Prince of the Tabernacle |
| 23° Chief of the Tabernacle |
| 22° Prince of Libanus |
| 21° Patriarch Noachite |
| 20° Master Ad Vitam |
| 19° Grand Pontiff |
| 18° Knight of the Rose Croix of H.R.D.M. |
| 17° Knight of the East and West |
| 16° Prince of Jerusalem |
| 15° Knight of the East or Sword |
| 14° Grand Elect Mason |
| 13° Master of the Ninth Arch |
| 12° Grand Master Architect |
| 11° Sublime Master Elected |
| 10° Elect of Fifteen |
| 9° Master Elect of Nine |
| 8° Intendent of the Building |
| 7° Provost and Judge |
| 6° Intimate Secretary |
| 5° Perfect Master |
| 4° Secret Master |

—Shrine◄—

Super Excellent Master
Select Master
Royal Master

ALLIED ORGANIZATIONS

Grotto
Tall Cedars of Lebanon
Eastern Star
Job's Daughters
Rainbow Girls
DeMolay

YORK RITE

Order of Knights Templar

Order of Knights of Malta

Order of Red Cross

Royal Arch Mason

Most Excellent Master

Past Master (Virtual)

Mark Master

3° Master Mason

2° Fellow Craft

1° Entered Apprentice

The Masonic Structure in the United States

PREFACE

Many Americans view the Masonic order as a benevolent and charitable fraternity, somehow based on the Bible, which conducts secret rituals in its temples and cements the loyalty of its initiates through certain passwords, oaths, handshakes, and symbols. The lodge does not seem much different from the Rotary and Lions clubs in their hometowns.

But the majority of Christians around the world, including at least ninety million in the United States, belong to churches that forbid or discourage Masonic membership.

Why? That is the question this book seeks to answer.

Several excellent books by English scholars in this field have been published since then, such as *Darkness Visible and Christian by Degrees*, by Walton Hannah. Father Hannah was then an Anglican priest in England and later a Roman Catholic priest in Canada. Another first-rate contribution is *The Nature of Freemasonry*, by Dr. Hubert S. Box, an Anglican theologian. All three of these books are valuable additions to the literature but are mainly concerned with English Masonry.

We have not undertaken this present study in order to irritate members of the lodge or to satisfy the mere curiosity of the "profane", as non-Masons are called by the brothers. We do believe that both Masons and others are entitled to a reasonable explanation for the attitude of the many Christian bodies that oppose the lodge.

No one can understand Catholicism without becoming

familiar with the Mass. No one can really know spiritualism without attending a séance, or fundamentalism without going to a revival. Likewise, a student of Freemasonry must understand the rituals of initiation into the three degrees if he would grasp the essence of Freemasonry. The rituals are presented in chapter 3 because they, better than any Masonic commentaries, give us an insight into the principles of the lodge.

Insofar as possible we have allowed Masons to speak for themselves in this book. We have relied heavily on three of the foremost authorities on Masonry in this country: Albert Pike, Dr. Albert Mackey, and Henry Wilson Coil. Pike (1809–1891) remodeled the entire structure of the Scottish rite and served as Sovereign Grand Commander of the Southern Jurisdiction from 1859 until his death. Mackey (1807–1881) gave the Craft a library of basic books, including his *Encyclopedia of Freemasonry, The Symbolism of Free-masonry, Mackey's Masonic Ritualist, Lexicon of Freemasonry,* and *Text Book of Masonic Jurisprudence.* Coil (1885–1974) edited the massive *Coil's Masonic Encyclopedia,* which was published in 1961. No other American Masons have had more influence and prestige than this trio.

Mackey erred, however, when he wrote in his *Encyclope-dia,* "The truth is that men who are not Masons never read authentic Masonic works. They have no interest in the topics discussed, and could not understand them, from a want of the preparatory education which the Lodge alone can supply. Therefore, were a writer even to trench a little on what may be considered as being really the arcana of Masonry, there is no danger of his thus making an improper revelation to improper persons."[1] On the contrary, this "improper"

[1] Albert G. Mackey, *Enyclopedia of Freemasonry* (Philadelphia: L. H. Everts), p. 617.

person has long had an interest in the topics discussed and has discovered innumerable corroborative bits of evidence in Masonic monitors, encyclopedias, speeches, commentaries, lectures, and histories.

The Masonic hierarchy does not encourage debate about the lodge. In a popular booklet, first published in 1955 and reprinted in 1984 by the Masonic Service Association, the question is asked, "What discussion of Masonry is proper in the presence of those not Masons?" The answer in part is: "As little as possible, unless in answer to a direct and respectful question the answer to which is not secret. . . . No argument should ever be held with anyone regarding Masonry. . . . Freemasonry needs no defense from anyone. The less Masonic matters are discussed in public, the better for Masonry." [2]

Besides the writings of Masons and critics of Masonry, we have consulted the various exposés written by disgruntled and disillusioned Masons. These range from the Morgan exposé through that of the evangelist and Oberlin College president Charles Finney to modern revelations, including those of Protestant ministers who have renounced the lodge. With the proper precautions, these exposés can be of considerable value, even though Masonic publications follow the simple policy of flatly denying their authenticity and impugning the integrity of the defectors. The trivial variations among the rituals of the dozens of Grand Lodges can be produced to discredit before naïve brethren any particular pirated ritual.

Masons themselves often own and use little cipher books, known as *Ecce Orienti* or *King Solomon's Temple*, which present the degree workings in a simple cryptography— much easier to decipher than most crossword puzzles. These

---

[2] *One Hundred One Questions about Freemasonry* (Silver Springs, Md.: Masonic Service Association, 1955), p. 65.

can be obtained by mail from Masonic publishers or purchased without show of credentials at many large bookstores. Furthermore, unsympathetic or careless widows of members are likely to offer their husbands' Masonic libraries to secondhand dealers and booksellers, and some such collections have even found their way to the shelves of Catholic university libraries. Black Masons who belong to lodges that white Masons brand as "clandestine" have no difficulty in obtaining genuine rituals for their own use. If there is one secret in Masonry, it is that there are no secrets.

Finally, we have obtained the wholehearted cooperation of three former Masons who are now active Catholic laymen. Two of these men were 32nd-degree members in the Scottish rite, and one served as Master of his lodge. The third reached the Order of Knights Templar in the York rite. Each has checked the chapters on the Blue Lodge initiation and on the Scottish and York rites. We have agreed to spare them any possible harassment by their former brethren by not divulging their names. Their assistance, however, is deeply appreciated.

Dr. Paul M. Bretscher of Concordia Seminary in Saint Louis, then chairman of the Commission on Fraternal Organizations of the Lutheran Church—Missouri Synod, graciously consented to review the entire manuscript of the original edition. His suggestions and comments have been invaluable. I would also like to thank Father Walton Hannah, Father John A. Hardon, S.J., Father Leo Piguet, Rev. Harold F. Roellig, Rev. E. P. Weber, and Rev. Philip Lochhaas.

Finally I would like to thank a number of Masonic friends and correspondents who have provided information and assisted in my research. They are Lt. Col. Harvey N. Brown (ret.), Dr. Mervin Hogan, Allen E. Roberts, Rev. Robert Uzzell, and Joseph A. Walkes, Jr. We have agreed to disagree.

I hasten to add that none of these gentlemen was asked to review the material on the rituals or to provide any information that would have violated his Masonic obligations.

> I am the way, and the truth, and the life;
> no one comes to the Father, but by me.
> —John 14:6

CHAPTER I

AMERICAN FREEMASONRY

Majority of World's Masons Live in the United States

About 2,100,000 American men belong to the Masonic order, the largest and oldest secret fraternal society. Another quarter of a million meet in the lodges of the predominantly black Prince Hall Masonry.

Some Masons take their membership very seriously. They attend meetings of their Blue Lodges, collect additional degrees in the Scottish and York rites, read Masonic books and periodicals, and try to internalize the principles of the Craft. Others, the great majority in this country, joined the lodge for business or social reasons and rarely if ever participate in Masonic activities. Freemasonry sets no attendance requirements such as those in the Rotary or Lions clubs; a Mason may be initiated, pay his annual dues, wear a Masonic ring or emblem, and never darken a lodge door for decades.

The Roman Catholic Church, Eastern Orthodoxy, and many Protestant churches also take the lodge seriously, so seriously that a Catholic who joins the Masonic lodge is said to be in a state of "serious sin" and may not receive the Eucharist. For hundreds of thousands of men, Freemasonry prescribes a specific philosophy of life, and the churches will not trivialize the lodge by suggesting that a Christian can remain a Mason provided he does not take his Masonry seriously. Masonry deserves to be judged by its basic principles and by its dedicated members, not by the majority who give little thought to the religious aspects of the lodge.

Masons as well as Catholics know of the historic antagonism between the two societies, Church and lodge, but few seem to know the reasons for the attitude of the Church. Some Masons attribute the Church's ban to some ancient political quarrel or imagine that the ban has something to do with the confessional. Too many Catholics are content to know that the Church forbids membership in the lodge without bothering to investigate the reasons behind this absolute prohibition.

Most U.S. Masons can probably testify that they have never heard any criticism of Roman Catholicism or other churches in their lodge meetings. The basic Blue Lodge forbids discussions about religion and politics, and rarely is this rule violated.

Thousands of Freemasons entertain kindly feelings toward the Church, support her hospitals and social-welfare institutions, and may even enroll their children in parochial schools. They see no reason why the Church should single out their lodge for condemnation, since they avoid discussing religion in the lodge room, open their temples to men of all faiths, and try to live good Christian lives themselves. They are usually convinced that the popes have been misled regarding the nature of Anglo-Saxon Freemasonry and that the ecclesiastical penalties should apply only to Catholics who join the admittedly political and anticlerical Grand Orients of Europe and Latin America. They see no essential differences between their lodge and the local Knights of Columbus council, and they wonder if this is not just another example of clerical intolerance.

These men of good will deserve a calm explanation of the

position of the Church. We will attempt to outline the chief reasons for the penalty that the Church attaches to lodge membership and to explain why the Church must oppose the basis of the Masonic system. A chapter will be devoted to a survey of Latin and European Masonry, but we will concentrate on the Masonic lodge in the U.S.

Masons generally define Masonry as a system of morality veiled in allegory and illustrated by symbols. The chief allegory, which forms the basis of the 3rd, or Master Mason's, degree, is that of Hiram Abiff (Huram-abi; cf. 2 Chron 2:13f.). Hiram appears briefly in the biblical description of the building of King Solomon's Temple, but Masonry has added a legend about his assassination and burial that becomes the death-and-resurrection rite of the degree.

Through the ages, some people have thought that the answers to the great mysteries of life could be found in secret societies. Through their initiation into such a society, they too could discover the answers withheld from the mass of mankind. The society guarded these secrets from the profane or outsiders and passed them along from one generation to the next.

Modern Masonry dates from 1717, when four Craft lodges gathered in a London tavern and set up a constitution for Free and Accepted Masons. These nonworking, or "honorary", Masons eventually took over the decadent lodges of working masons and developed the system of speculative Masonry we know today. We will discuss the origin of the lodge at greater detail in the following chapter.

Today, Masonry enrolls almost all of its estimated four million members in the United States and British Commonwealth nations and claims small constituencies in other countries. In many American communities, particularly in the South and Midwest, the local lodge forms a sort of pan–Protestant men's fellowship; membership in the lodge is considered a certificate of bourgeois respectability. As we shall see, a large number of Protestant and Eastern Orthodox bodies continue to oppose the lodge, but the main Protestant denominations—Methodist, Baptist, Presbyterian, Episcopal—offer no official objection to dual membership in the lodge and the Christian Church. The lodge demands only belief in God and in the immortality of the soul.

Masonic authorities are unable to agree on the precise number of "landmarks", the Masonic name for the essential points of the Craft. However, Anglo-Saxons usually include the following landmarks in any listing: the modes of recognition, including signs, grips, and passwords; the three-degree system, including the Royal Arch; the Hiramic legend of the third degree; belief in a Supreme Architect and in a future life; the right of any Master Mason to visit any regular lodge; the use of the Volume of the Sacred Law; the equality of all members of the lodge; secrecy; and the symbolic method of teaching.

Masonry bars most people from its ranks. No women, minors, atheists, or paupers may discover its "secrets". In the U.S. only a handful of blacks have been initiated into any of the sixteen thousand regular lodges; the Prince Hall lodges, which date back to 1775, are considered clandestine and irregular by white Masons.

Masonic affiliation has held a great appeal to men seeking political office. In fact, fourteen U.S. presidents have been Master Masons: Washington, Monroe, Jackson, Polk, Buchanan, Johnson, Garfield, McKinley, Theodore Roosevelt, Taft, Harding, Franklin D. Roosevelt, Truman, and Ford. Truman, once the Grand Master of Masons of Missouri, was the last Master Mason elected to the presidency; Johnson received the Entered Apprentice degree in 1937 but never went on to the third, or Master Mason, degree; and Ford, of course, was not elected president. Eisenhower, Nixon, Kennedy, Carter, Reagan, and Clinton reached the White House without Masonic membership.

Some chief executives have been bitter critics of secret societies. For example, John Quincy Adams wrote: "I am prepared to complete the demonstration before God and man, that the Masonic oath, obligations and penalties cannot possibly be reconciled to the laws of morality, of Christianity, or of the land." Millard Fillmore warned: "The Masonic fraternity tramples upon our rights, defeats the administration of justice, and bids defiance to every government which it cannot control."

At one time the great majority of members of Congress identified themselves as Masons. For example, in 1923 some three hundred out of 435 members of the House of Representatives were Masons, as were thirty of forty-eight senators. By 1984 only fifty-one House members and fourteen senators belonged to the lodge. Among the remaining senators in the Craft at this writing are Robert Byrd, John Glenn, Jesse Helms, and Strom Thurmond.

Masonic dominance of the U.S. Supreme Court has been documented by Paul A. Fisher in his book *Behind the Lodge Door*. Between 1949 and 1956 eight of the nine justices were Masons; by 1981 this had dropped to one.[1] The most recent Mason to be appointed to the Court was Thurgood Marshall in 1967; he was a member of the black Prince Hall lodge.

Teddy Roosevelt joined the lodge only after he became vice president. Taft, like Generals George C. Marshall and Douglas MacArthur, was made a Mason "at sight". This means that a state Grand Master dispenses with the formalities

---

[1] Paul A. Fisher, *Behind the Lodge Door* (Washington, D.C.: Shield, 1988), appendix A.

of filing a petition and the usual waiting period between the conferral of degrees. All Grand Masters have the prerogative of making others Masons at sight but seldom exercise it.

Harding became an Entered Apprentice in 1901 but did not become a Master Mason until 1920. By the time he died as president three years later, he had become a 32nd-degree Scottish rite Mason and a Shriner. His administration marked the high-water mark for Masonic influence in the political life of the nation, but the scandals and corruption of the Harding administration brought no credit to the lodge.

Some idea of the prestige of Masonry may be gained by a brief look at the caliber of men who have knocked at Masonry's doors. They include Benjamin Franklin (who helped initiate Voltaire into the lodge), Paul Revere, John Jacob Astor, Mark Twain, Henry Ford, Will Rogers, Henry Clay, John Philip Sousa, Sam Houston, Irving Berlin, Luther Burbank, Samuel Gompers, Charles Lindbergh, and J. Edgar Hoover. FDR defeated three brother (Republican) Masons in his campaigns for the presidency: Alfred M. Landon, Wendell Willkie, and Thomas E. Dewey.

Masonry was transplanted to American shores from England about a dozen years after the founding of the first Grand Lodge. The Duke of Norfolk appointed Daniel Coxe to be the first Provincial Grand Master in North America in 1730.

Many of the leaders of the American Revolution, such as Washington and Franklin, were Masons, but according to the Masonic writer Charles Van Cott, more Masons remained loyal to the crown than to the colonial cause, and at the start of the revolt only one of the one hundred or so lodges sided with the patriots.[2] Washington joined the

[2] Charles Van Cott, *Freemasonry: A Sleeping Giant* (Minneapolis: T. S. Denison & Co., 1959), p. 108.

Masonic order in 1752 and at the time of his election as president was serving as Master of his lodge. Benedict Arnold was also a Mason.

Masonic orators and writers sometimes get carried away and assert that most of the signers of the Declaration of Independence were Masons, but the evidence of Masonic affiliation for many of these signers is flimsy or nonexistent. A publication of the Masonic Service Association identifies only nine of the fifty-six signers as Freemasons, and some historians put the figure at eight.[3]

Many of the founders of the Republic were Deists rather than orthodox Christians. Deism, a product of the Enlightenment, maintained that everything could be known by reason alone, and it acknowledged no debt to divine revelation. The God of the Deists was the master clock builder who wound up the universe and watched it tick away. He could also be viewed as the Great Architect, so it was understandable that many Deists found the religious and philosophical stance of Freemasonry to be congenial. Neither Thomas Paine nor Thomas Jefferson was a Freemason, but as Deists they shared the rationalist orientation of the Craft; some have called them "Masons without aprons".

By the end of the American Revolution, Masonic lodges were flourishing and enjoyed the prestige of Washington and other national heroes who had been Masons. But Masonic growth was abruptly halted by the Morgan incident.

A thirty-eight-foot monument in Batavia, New York, has been erected to the memory of Morgan. The inscription at the foot of the monument reads: "Sacred to the memory of Wm. Morgan, a native of Virginia, a captain in the War of 1812, a respectable citizen of Batavia, and a martyr to the

[3] *Masonic Signers of the Declaration* (Silver Springs, Md.: Masonic Service Association, 1975), p. 4.

freedom of writing, printing and speaking the truth. He was abducted from near this spot in the year 1826, by Freemasons, and murdered for revealing the secrets of their order."

Morgan had written an exposé of the lodge that so angered the Masons in the vicinity that they kidnapped the author and took him to Fort Niagara. He was never again seen alive, but a body was later identified as his, and the general public concluded that for once Masons had taken their obligation to protect their secrets and punish offenders in a serious rather than a symbolic sense. Three men were eventually given prison terms for their part in the affair, while Masons have believed that Morgan escaped from his captors and became a missing rather than a murdered person. William Preston Vaughn, in his book *The Antimasonic Party in the United States, 1826-1843*, concludes that "Morgan was probably murdered by misguided Masons."

As a result of this scandal, the Anti-Masonic political party was formed, which polled 128,000 votes in the 1830 election and carried Vermont in the campaign against Jackson in 1832. Leaders of the Anti-Masonic Party were Thurlow Weed, William H. Seward, William Wirt, and Thaddeus Stevens. Rhode Island and Vermont passed laws against the oaths demanded by secret societies. Thousands who had joined the lodge for business and social advantages burned their aprons; membership in the New York lodges dropped from twenty thousand to three thousand in a few years. Associations of Protestant churches denounced all secret societies; hundred of lodges dissolved, and 140 anti-Masonic periodicals began publication as a direct result of the Morgan incident. But anti-Masonry as a political force in this country was dead by 1832.

The Morgan incident did slow Masonic growth in this country, and Masonry's expansion did not resume until after the Civil War. Neither Lincoln nor Grant was a Mason, nor was Jefferson Davis or Robert E. Lee.

A former Confederate general and Freemason, Nathan Bedford Forrest, founded the Ku Klux Klan and served as its first Imperial Wizard. Albert Pike held the office of Chief Justice of the Ku Klux Klan while he was simultaneously Sovereign Grand Commander of the Scottish rite, Southern Jurisdiction. Pike's racism was well known. He expressed his concept of Masonic brotherhood succinctly: "I took my obligation to white men, not to negroes. When I have to accept negroes as brothers or leave Masonry, I shall leave it." Some believe Pike concocted the ritual for the original KKK.

For most U.S. secret societies, the period between 1870 and 1930 was their period of greatest growth. Not only the Masonic lodges but the Knights of Phythias and the Odd Fellows (sometimes known as the poor man's Masonry) enjoyed significant membership gains. Freemasonry ingratiated itself with mainline Protestant churches and denied or downplayed its religious character. The lodge seemed to foster the same virtues of industry, thrift, honesty, and sobriety that characterized white middle-class Protestants. The lodges courted Protestant ministers, marched to church services in a body, and assured prospective members that Masonry, at least in the U.S., was squarely based on the Holy Bible.

Some sociologists attributed the spectacular expansion of fraternal organizations in this country during these decades to the barrenness of Calvinist worship and the absence of royalty and its attendant ceremonials. Some said the matriarchal influences in the society drove the men into lodges where they could bar all women, exchange secret passwords and grips, assume outlandish titles, and participate in the secret and manly rituals.

A dedicated Mason, William Joseph Simmons, revived the Ku Klux Klan in 1915, and in the following years the Klan achieved members and power that far eclipsed the success of the original Klan. By the mid-1920s, the KKK controlled some states, such as Indiana, from the courthouse to the statehouse. Almost all of the top officials of the revived Klan were also Masons.[4]

Enthusiasm for the Klan was more widespread among average Masons than among Grand Masters and Masonic leaders, who saw the dangers of too close an association with such an unsavory group. But Klan recruiters concentrated on Masons, since they believed that they were already hostile toward Catholics and blacks and not overly fond of Jews. As one historian wrote:

> The Klan shared its Protestant restrictiveness with the Masons and more than once sought to capitalize on the parallel. Kleagles commonly remarked to prospects, in an offhand manner, that "the Klan is, in fact, a Masonic movement." Many leading Klansmen, in both the old Klan and the new, were Masons; [Hiram] Evans himself had gained the 32nd degree.[5]

Another historian of the Klan commented:

> Wherever possible, F. Y. Clarke [a Klan leader] selected his salesmen from among members of other lodges, since they would be likely to be skilled in the world of ritualism and fraternal dynamics. He particularly favored Masons because of the size of their own order and because

[4] For further information on the relationship of Masonry and the Ku Klux Klan, see William J. Whalen, *Handbook of Secret Organizations* (Milwaukee: Bruce, 1966), pp. 91–100.

[5] William Pierce Randel, *The Ku Klux Klan* (Philadelphia: Chilton, 1965), p. 200. Copyright © 1965 by the author. Reprinted with the permission of the publisher, Chilton Book Company, Radnor, Pa.

the chances were they would not be overly friendly toward Roman Catholics. Many Masonic leaders bitterly denounced and fought the Klan both for its divisive effects within their lodges and because they disapproved of violent intolerance. However, the rank and file turned to the Klan by the thousands, and the Scottish Rite Mason and Orange Lodges were particularly rich hunting grounds.[6]

A third student of fraternalism observed:

Another indication that Masons were susceptible to the racism and anti-Semitism of the period [1920s] was the popularity of the Ku Klux Klan with Masons. Although no reliable figure exists, the KKK appears to have been quite successful in recruiting Masons to its ranks. . . . While its influence in local lodges probably varied widely, the infiltration of the Klan was noticeable enough that most Grand Masters, prompted by unfavorable public opinion and dismay over the dissension the Klan was promoting within Masonry, found it necessary to make a statement either condemning the Ku Klux Klan or denying Masonry's connection with it.[7]

One convert to Ku Kluxism was Hugo Black, who eventually became a justice of the U.S. Supreme Court. In her memoirs of her husband, Black's widow explains: "The Klan in Alabama, Hugo said, was organized largely by Masons and he had been a Mason since he was twenty-one years old."[8]

[6] David M. Chalmers, *Hooded Americanism* (New York: Doubleday, 1965), p. 34.
[7] Lynn Dumenil, *Freemasonry and American Culture* (Princeton, N.J.: Princeton University Press, 1984), pp. 122–23. Copyright © 1984 by Princeton University Press and reprinted by permission.
[8] *Mr. Justice and Mrs. Black: The Memoirs of Hugo L. Black and Elizabeth Black* (New York: Random House, 1986), p. 70.

The caution of a number of Grand Masters was well founded, and when the Ku Klux Klan collapsed in a storm of corruption, murder, rape, and torture, the Grand Lodges, if not the rank-and-file Masons, could point to their warnings against entangling the lodge with the Klan. At the same time, it must be said that the anti-Catholic, anti-black, and anti-Semitic orientation of the KKK often matched that of the ordinary Mason in the 1920s and explained the magnetic appeal of the Invisible Empire.

The level of anti-Catholic attacks reached new highs in Masonic as well as Klan publications in the 1920s. Dumenil writes: "In Masonic literature, anti-Catholic rhetoric was far more pervasive than it had been in the late nineteenth century. Masons continued to describe Catholicism as the enemy of Freemasonry, but by far the most persistent theme was Catholicism as an enemy of democracy."[9]

For decades the *New Age*, official magazine of the Southern Jurisdiction of the Scottish rite, carried on an aggressive campaign against Roman Catholicism, its popes and bishops, its parochial schools, and its alleged designs on American democracy. The comments of John B. Reynolds, a regular contributor, are typical: "Masonry needs no defense and attacks no one. To paraphrase Thomas Jefferson, Masonry will always fight for freedom from tyranny over the minds of men, be it political or clerical. The Roman Catholic hierarchy represents both; it boldly so states, and we know it."[10] The *Scottish Rite Journal*, known as the *New Age* from 1903 to 1990, goes monthly to all Scottish rite Masons in thirty-three southern and western states.

In particular, the lodges saw the parochial school as a tool of an undemocratic hierarchy. In Oregon in 1922, the Ku

[9] Dumenil, *Freemasonry*, p. 124.
[10] *New Age*, June 1965.

Klux Klan and the Scottish rite Masons were instrumental in getting an initiative on the ballot that would make attendance at a public school compulsory between the ages of eight and sixteen. Both the Oregon and the U.S. Supreme Courts declared the law unconstitutional.

Some Masons worried about the alliance of the lodge and the Klan, and the Grand Master of Oregon said that the initiative did not have Grand Lodge approval. But Dumenil explains:

> It is unlikely that many Masons opposed the bill because of its unfair impact on parochial schools. Historians who have argued that Masonry was a dupe of the Ku Klux Klan on this issue have not recognized that Masonry's support of public schools and opposition to parochial ones was not at all unique to the Oregon situation. Although the Oregon legislation was exceptional, the sentiments behind the bill—an antipathy to Catholicism and a desire to fuse a homogeneous society by means of public education—were consistent with Masonic principles throughout the country.[11]

By the mid-1920s the Masonic lodges reported more than three million members, and this at a time when the population was about half of what it is today. This was the heyday of Freemasonry and most of the other secret fraternal organizations. Some would disappear or linger for a few decades. Masonry would never again enroll the same percentage of white adult males as it did in 1925. With the Depression, hundreds of thousands of Masons quit paying dues, and social forces during the 1940s and 1950s worked against revival of interest in the lodges.

America's leaders during World War II, Roosevelt and Truman, were both Freemasons, as was the British prime

[11] Dumenil, *Freemasonry*, p. 144.

minister, Churchill. Shortly after Pearl Harbor, Earl Warren, attorney general of California and past Grand Master of Masons in that state, urged that all Japanese Americans, citizens or aliens, be sent to "relocation centers" for the duration of the war. Warren became Chief Justice of the U.S. Supreme Court in 1953.

During World War I, the major welfare programs for servicemen were conducted by the Knights of Columbus. The Masons, fragmented into individual state Grand Lodges, did not seem to be able to come up with a program the armed forces and the federal government could support. To remedy this situation, the Masonic Service Association set up a department of welfare in 1940 to establish Masonic service centers for men in uniform. To pay for these centers, each of the nation's two-and-a-half million Masons was asked to contribute the modest sum of ten cents.[12] After the war, American Masons raised $123,000, which they sent to help beleaguered European Masons.

Naturally, the Southern Jurisdiction viewed the election of a Roman Catholic to the presidency as a clear and present danger to the republic and urged Scottish rite Masons to alert their friends and neighbors about the perils of a Kennedy victory in 1960. Luther A. Smith, Sovereign Grand Commander of the Scottish rite, Southern Jurisdiction, told the readers of the *New Age* that

> whatever bigotry is in evidence in the United States is exhibited solely by the Roman Catholic hierarchy; that the Canon Law of the Roman Church and the directives of the Pope validate the fears of the people that the dual allegiance of American Catholics is a present danger to our free institutions, and lastly that the people in passing

[12] Allen E. Roberts, *Brother Truman* (Highland Springs, Va.: Anchor Communications, 1985), p. 73.

upon the qualifications of a Catholic candidate for the Presidency will be guided by their knowledge of history and their great store of plain old-fashioned common horse sense, and their innate caution not to gamble when their liberties and the national security are at stake.

Among American citizens there should be no question or suspicion of allegiance to any foreign power, but in the case of the Roman Catholic citizen, his church is the guardian of his conscience and asserts that he must obey its laws and decrees even if they are in conflict with the Constitution and laws of the United States.[13]

Unlike the Blue Lodges, the Scottish rite has never felt constrained to avoid discussions of politics and religion in its publications and deliberations.

However, during the same presidential campaign, the head of the Northern Masonic Scottish Rite Jurisdiction, George E. Bushnell, banned all political material from Scottish rite magazines. In an interview, Bushnell, a former supreme court justice in Michigan, said, "A man who would urge Senator Kennedy's defeat because of his religion has entirely forgotten the principles of American government. If men of the Catholic Faith are willing to die for our flag, certainly their faith should be no barrier to their serving as commander-in-chief of our forces as President."

The structure of Freemasonry has not changed over the years. Every Mason in good standing belongs to a Blue Lodge; maintenance of membership in this lodge is essential to keeping membership in any of the so-called higher rites or the Shrine. No one outranks the Master of his lodge or the Grand Master in his state. A 33rd-degree Mason would always rank below the Grand Master of his state even though the latter might be only a Master Mason.

[13] *New Age*, February 1960.

Blue Lodges in each state of the union, the District of Columbia, and Puerto Rico are grouped in Grand Lodges. In most countries, Grand Lodges are national bodies, but all attempts to form such a nationwide Grand Lodge of the United States have failed. The principles of Masonry do not vary from Grand Lodge to Grand Lodge, but details of ritual and Masonic law do differ.

Some students of fraternalism, Masons and non-Masons, estimate that 90 percent of the lodge's initiates take no further interest in the Blue Lodges. The routine of initiating new members through memorized rituals, which forms much of the activity of a Blue Lodge, seems to have less and less appeal to the diploma elite in the 1990s.

A minority of Master Masons continue into the "higher degrees". A Mason can climb one or both Masonic ladders as his spare time and pocketbook dictate: the Scottish or York rites. The former consists of twenty-nine degrees superimposed on the basic three, plus the active and honorary 33rd degree. The York or American rite leads to membership in the Knights Templar, which is limited to Christian Masons. Knights Templar and 32nd-degree Masons are eligible to join the Shrine, Masonry's fun organization.

An organization dedicated to brotherhood, Masonry ironically has been a bulwark of racial segregation in the United States. By 1998, decades after most American institutions had accepted racial integration, the Grand Lodges could count very few black members in their jurisdictions. As the author of a recent scholarly study of black Freemasonry observes, "The legitimation of social intermingling between black and white Masons has remained anathema in mainstream Freemasonry." [14]

[14] Loretta J. Williams, *Black Freemasonry and Middle-Class Realities* (Columbia, Mo.: University of Missouri Press, 1980), p. 98.

A lodge within the British military forces initiated Prince Hall with fourteen free black men in 1775 after the men had been rebuffed in their attempt to join Saint John's lodge in Boston. Eventually the black Masons received a charter from the Grand Master of the Grand Lodge of England for African Lodge No. 459 (1784). Regular Masonry has continued to deny recognition to Prince Hall lodges, and individual lodges have barred black candidates by the simple method of the black cube.

Except for one curious exception, Alpha Lodge No. 116 in New Jersey, regular Freemasonry remains ninety-nine and forty-four hundredths percent white. In most states a Prince Hall Mason may not visit a white lodge, nor a white Mason visit a Prince Hall lodge, without risking Masonic punishment. Albert Pike, no friend of blacks, admitted in 1875: "Prince Hall lodge was as regular a lodge as any lodge created by competent authority. It had a perfect right to establish other lodges and make itself a Mother Lodge."

When the Grand Lodge of New Jersey accepted several blacks into membership, other Grand Lodges decried the action, and some severed fraternal relations with New Jersey. Mississippi was one. The Grand Master of that state wrote in 1908:

> Masonry never contemplated that her privileges should be extended to a race, totally, morally and intellectually incapacitated to discharge the obligations which they assume or have conferred upon them in a Masonic lodge. It is no answer that there are exceptions to this general character of the race. We legislate for the race and not for the exceptions. We hold that affiliation with negroes is contrary to the teachings of Masonry, and is dangerous to the interest of the Fraternity of Free and Accepted Masons.

Racism is only one of several factors that have led to a dramatic membership decline of Masonry in this country. American men find far more activities competing for their spare time than they did seventy years ago. Many young men would rather spend their time with their families or in church and community projects than in attending lodge meetings.

Had the Masonic lodges enrolled the same percentage of adult white males in the mid-1990s as they did in the 1920s, they would be reporting more than twelve million members instead of fewer than 2,200,000. In fact, the lodges lost nearly half of their members between 1959 and 1995. In recent years the lodges have declined by about 2 percent each year, and Masonry's future in the next century seems uncertain.

Along with California, Ohio, and Pennsylvania, the Grand Lodge of Texas reports one of the largest numbers of Masons of any state. The *Texas Monthly* published an article in 1983 entitled "Slow Nights at the Grand Lodge". The writer extolled the role of Freemasonry in the history of that state but concluded:

> Unless enrollment trends change soon, by the turn of the century few Masons will be left in Texas. The number of people who ask to join has been declining in both [regular and Prince Hall] orders since the years immediately following World War II. Today there are about 19,000 Prince Hall Masons in Texas, nearly 20 percent fewer than five years ago. Last year alone 600 Prince Hall members died, nearly 3 percent of the total. The Waco Grand Lodge has 209,000 members, down from a peak of 245,000 in 1961. Current annual enlistment of 3,000 Masons doesn't replace the 5,000 members who die each year. Perhaps most significant, the group's prestige is slipping.[15]

---

[15] *Texas Monthly*, December 1983, p. 120.

No doubt one reason for the decline in interest in Masonry has been the expansion of the many service clubs such as Rotary, Optimist, Exchange, Kiwanis, and Lions. Attuned to commerce and business, these clubs are relatively simple to join; new members need not memorize lengthy rituals and endure drawn-out initiations. Rotary and other clubs actually seek out new members, while Freemasonry supposedly waits for the candidate to take the initiative to join. Service clubs enforce attendance requirements; no one can remain a member of a Lions club, for example, and not show up for meetings for years at a time. The clubs provide many opportunities for committee work and participation. Finally, the clubs provide variety in their meetings, usually a short talk on some subject of current interest. The Blue Lodges have been unable to compete successfully with the service clubs for the time of their members.

At one time in small-town America, the local Masonic lodge provided some measure of fellowship and a break from the daily routine of work. Today other attractions, especially for younger men, far outweigh the lure of the lodge. The college graduates in their twenties and thirties who would be Masonry's natural recruits seem to prefer spending their free time jogging, watching television, attending sports events, reading, doing church work, listening to music, participating in their service club, working around the house, and helping take care of the kids to spending hours in the lodge hall.

Many societal changes have worked against the lodge. For example, surveys now indicate that about 37 percent of college students in this country identify themselves as Roman Catholics; fifty years ago this figure was closer to 10 percent. If you add the college graduates who are Lutherans, Mormons, conservative Protestants, and atheists to the number of Roman Catholics, you find that more than half of these men are unlikely to take any interest in Freemasonry.

The typical lodge meeting attracts only a small percentage of the dues-paying membership, and with good reason. Most people do not want to see a play more than once, and the main business of the lodges is to initiate new members using the same memorized ritual week after week. Van Cott writes: "The members of the Lodge are tired of watching third-rate actors, out of character, out of time, muttering the same old stuff." [16] No casual Mason, Frank S. Land founded the Order of DeMolay and was ex-Imperial Potentate of the Shrine. Yet Land complained: "Ninety-two per cent of those who take the first three degrees come back once or twice and never come back again." [17] But Masonry has no mechanism to refurbish its ritual to retain the interest of the majority of its adherents.

Some Masons keep paying their dues long after they have dropped out of active participation because of the benevolent activities of the lodge. Either they channel charitable contributions through their lodge, or they hope that their brothers and the lodge will be there to help them in times of trouble. Grand Lodges in twenty-nine states operate homes for elderly Masons and their wives or widows. Only Masons in good standing are eligible to receive any assistance. The individual Mason has no *quid pro quo* share in such assistance, since the Masonic lodge, unlike, say, the Knights of Columbus, does not operate an insurance program.

The Masonic lodges in the United States enroll some of the finest gentlemen in the nation. We will try to show that a person cannot be a thoughtful Christian and a thoughtful Mason, but we will never question the sincerity of anyone

[16] Van Cott, *Freemasonry*, p. 155.
[17] Quoted by Van Cott, ibid., p. 153.

who claims to be both; we must question his consistency in giving allegiance to an exclusive religion such as Christianity and to the religion of naturalism propagated by the Masonic lodge. For many Masons, the influence of the lodge in their lives is slight; we have no way of measuring their degree of commitment to Masonic principles compared to their commitment to Jesus Christ. Certainly many "Christian Masons" display far more Christianity than Masonry in their daily lives.

CHAPTER II

ORIGIN OF MASONRY

English Grand Lodge Formed in Apple Tree Tavern

Masonry as we know it dates from 1717, but Masonic legends claim a much greater antiquity for the Craft. Many naïve and credulous members take those fanciful pretensions seriously and believe that Masonry can be traced back to King Solomon's Temple or to the Tower of Babel. One discredited Masonic historian, Dr. George Oliver, maintained that the lodge began with creation itself and that Adam was not only the first man but the first Masonic Grand Master. According to Oliver, this pure Masonry became corrupted at the time of the Tower of Babel but was rediscovered and purified by Saint John the Evangelist.

A candid appraisal of these fables is given by Delmer Darrah in his *History and Evolution of Freemasony*: "Masons have believed the things concerning the origin of the institution that they wanted to believe and have gone forth and told them as facts. When links were missing, they have been supplied by drawing upon fertile imaginations." [1]

He adds: "If there is in Freemasonry any similarity between its customs and those of the practices of several thousand years ago, it does not mean that Freemasonry has any

[1] Delmer Duane Darrah, *History and Evolution of Freemasonry* (Chicago: Charles T. Powner, 1951), pp. 25–26.

connection whatsoever with those rites but that they were woven into the fraternity in modern times with a view to enhancing the ritual and investing the fraternity with an atmosphere of antiquity."[2]

Masons are led to believe by their ritual and various commentaries that King Solomon, Hiram of Tyre, Hiram Abiff (Huram-abi), and Saint John the Evangelist were all active members of the lodge. Intelligent Masons, of course, know this for the spoof that it is, but many others never question the claim to antiquity. Their brethren, realizing the value of antiquity to *esprit de corps*, do not bother to disenchant them.

Modern Masonry has borrowed from many diverse traditions, such as those of the suppressed Knights Templar, the Roman Collegia of Artificers, the Jewish Kabbalists, the mystery cults, the Rosicrucians, and the operative masons of the Middle Ages. The Masonic historians Pick and Knight admit:

> Many of the doctrines or tenets inculcated in Freemasonry belong to the vast traditions of humanity of all ages and all parts of the world. Nevertheless, not only has no convincing evidence yet been brought forward to prove the lineal descent of our Craft from any ancient organization which is known to have, or even suspected of having, taught any similar system of morality, but also from what we know of the Craft in the few centuries prior to the formation of the first Grand Lodge in 1717, it is excessively unlikely that there was any such parentage.[3]

Of the various influences that contributed to the Masonic fraternity, the greatest was that of the working masons. Father Humphrey J. T. Johnston states: "Modern Freemasonry, the creation of Deists and Jews with a measure of

[2] Ibid., p. 36.
[3] Fred L. Pick and Norman G. Knight, *The Pocket History of Freemasonry* (New York: Philosophical Library, 1953), p. 9.

Huguenot assistance, built on a foundation provided by the old confraternities of stonemasons which in a degenerate form had survived the Reformation."[4]

These working masons, who built the magnificent cathedrals and castles of medieval Europe and were greatly esteemed for their know-how, served as apprentices and fellow craftsmen before qualifying as master masons. They devised a system of secret signs and grips that served the purpose of today's union card and identified the initiated as properly qualified workmen. Masons were forced to travel from place to place to pursue their occupation; membership in the powerful stonemasons' guild meant that a mason could rely on help from his brethren in difficult circumstances and in strange lands. He could likewise be counted upon to preserve trade secrets from outsiders.

After the Reformation had practically halted the construction of new church buildings, the waning masonic lodges began to admit "honorary" or nonworking members to their ranks. The original lodges were unquestionably orthodox in their adherence to the Catholic religion that they served so admirably. One of the earliest masonic charges reads: "The first charge is that you shall bee true man to God and holy church, and that you use no heresie or error by your understanding or by teachings of indiscreet men."

Eventually the honorary members outnumbered the operative masons, more or less dispossessed the active members, and took over the symbols and secret signs of the lodges to form what we know as speculative Masonry. Members were expected to believe in God and in the immortality of the soul, but otherwise their religious views were completely irrelevant to the lodge.

[4] Humphrey J. T. Johnston, *Freemasonry: A Short Historical Sketch* (London: Catholic Truth Society, 1952), p. 3.

In 1717 a governing authority known as the "Grand Lodge of England" was established at a meeting of four surviving lodges in the Apple Tree Tavern in London. Two Protestant clergymen, Dr. John Theophilus Desaguliers and Dr. James Anderson, were instrumental in setting up the self-styled governing body. Not all lodges were willing to submit to the rule of the new Grand Lodge, but by 1725 the original four lodges had grown to sixty-four, of which fifty were in London. The Craft captured the fancy of certain members of the English aristocracy after 1721, and they in turn were flattered by the brethren. The first royal Grand Master took office in that year, and this position has since then been reserved to a nobleman.

Originally, some lodges worked one degree, and others, two. The Hiramic legend that forms the basis for the present Master Mason degree was introduced by Anderson sometime after 1720; the three-degree system was not adopted until 1730.

Anderson prepared a new *Book of Constitutions* in 1723 that spelled out the new policy of the lodge toward religious affiliation.

> A Mason is obliged by his Tenure, to obey the Moral Law, and if he rightly understand the Art, he will never be a stupid Atheist nor an irreligious Libertine. But though in ancient times Masons were charged in every country to be of the Religion of that Country or Nation, whatever it was, yet 'tis now thought more expedient only to oblige them to that Religion in which all Men agree, leaving their particular opinions to themselves, that is, to be good Men and true, or Men of Honour and Honesty, by whatsoever Denominations or Persuasions they may be distinguished.

Obviously the religion to which masons in medieval times were expected to adhere was Roman Catholicism, since it was the religion of Europe. Obviously, too, the "Religion in which all Men agree" is not Catholicism or Christianity, since many men do not agree with the central theological positions of Christianity. These central beliefs are relegated to the role of "particular opinions".

This change in policy opened the door to membership by Jews, Deists, and Muslims but supposedly barred atheists and polytheists. Jews might well feel at home in the lodge, since the Hiram Abiff legend was built on the Old rather than the New Testament, and the Craft borrowed most of its terminology from the Hebrew scriptures. The core of Masonry, that mankind has suffered a great loss that eventually will be recovered, could easily be understood to mean the loss of the Temple and of Jewish nationhood.

Although the aristocrats took up the Masonic hobby, the lower classes often sneered at the Masonic folderol and snob appeal and enjoyed pelting participants in Masonic processions. The lodges continued to meet in taverns and were known as convivial associations. Before midcentury, the first published exposés began to appear.

Eventually a rival Grand Lodge was founded, which charged that the main body had de-Christianized the Craft, had transposed the modes of recognition in the first and second degrees, omitted certain prayers, ignored saints' days, and committed other crimes. The dissidents took the name "Antients" and labeled the original Grand Lodge the "Moderns". The rivalry continued from 1751 to 1813, when two royal brothers headed the opposing factions and agreed to sign the articles of reunion. The amalgamated Grand Lodge consented to include the Royal Arch degree favored by the Antients as a part of pure and ancient Masonry, although most Masons in England, as in America, never take this degree. The Antients compromised on every point in which they had claimed to uphold the Christian orientation of the Craft. Reunion of the Antients and Moderns in America followed the English reunion by four years.

From England, the Craft spread to the continent and to British colonies throughout the world, often serving as a handy instrument of British policy. Although the Church's basic objections to Masonry apply to all branches of the Craft, we can distinguish two main Masonic traditions: those of Anglo-Saxon Masonry, including England, Scotland, the United States, Holland, and the Scandinavian countries; and those of the Grand Orients such as France, Spain, Italy, and South America. We shall review the status of Latin and European Masonry in chapter 10. Suffice to say, the attitude of the Church toward the lodge meant that, in Catholic nations, only religious rebels and Jews sought admission to the lodges. This concentration of atheists, agnostics, free-thinkers, Jews, and anticlericals turned Latin Masonry into a subversive and hostile critic of Christianity and all religions. When the Grand Orient of France in 1877 rejected the landmark of belief in God and removed the Volume of the Sacred Law from the lodges, the Anglo-Saxons severed fraternal relations, which have never been resumed.

Latin Freemasonry grew increasingly revolutionary and anticlerical after 1860 but seems to be undergoing a process of disintegration today. English Freemasonry went on to become ultrarespectable, bourgeois, vaguely Protestant, and royalist. In the United States as well as in England, the lodge has assumed the proportions of a mass movement among the white Protestant middle class rather than an elite. The Catholic heritage of the operative Masonic lodges has been all but obliterated, and the brethren have long been nourished on a concoction of fables and falsehoods regarding the origin of the fraternity.

CHAPTER III

MASONIC INITIATION

Three Degrees Comprise the Blue Lodge

Candidates for the Masonic order must receive a series of three degrees before reaching full membership in the Blue Lodge; these are the basic degrees for all other Masonic honors. They are "entered" as Entered Apprentices, "passed" as Fellow Crafts, and "raised" as Master Masons in ceremonies on three separate evenings or occasions of meeting. Once Master Masons, they supposedly know all Masonic secrets, which will enable them to "travel and work in foreign countries and receive wages as such".

Each candidate petitions in writing for admittance and must be recommended by two members. Strictly speaking, he may not be prompted or solicited by Masonic friends or relatives. Actually, although the lodge abstains from membership campaigns and similar hoopla, most prospective members are sold on the advantages of affiliation by some other Mason. The writer has talked to Protestant ministers who revealed that they had been importuned several times in their careers to enter the lodge but, for religious reasons, regularly declined the invitations.

A duly assembled Masonic lodge consists of at least seven Freemasons acting under a warrant or dispensation from some Grand Lodge. They assemble in a lodge room on the

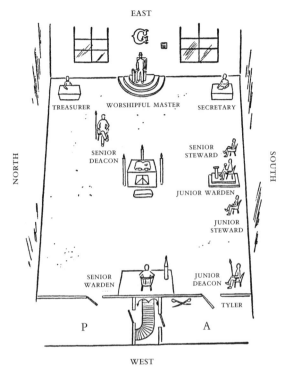

Floor plan of Masonic lodge, indicating position of officers.

second or third floor of a building well guarded against "cowans" (a Masonic term for eavesdroppers) and the non-Masonic "profane". When the candidate petitions for membership and submits his initiation fee, the Master, upon hearing the application read in meeting, appoints an Investigating Committee of three Masons to study the character of the applicant and to report at the next regular meeting. Favorable recommendations from at least two of the Investigating Committee are sufficient to bring the application to vote. If on the first ballot all balls or cubes are white (or "clear"), the candidate is declared elected to receive the degrees. If even one black ball or cube appears, the ballot is "cloudy", and it is necessary to vote a second time; and if on the second ballot a black ball appears, the candidate is rejected. A unanimous vote is required.

On the appointed night for conferring the First or Entered Apprentice Degree, the local lodge conducts a Lodge of Entered Apprentices. The usual officers include Master, Senior Warden, Junior Warden, Secretary, Treasurer, Senior Deacon, Junior Deacon, Senior and Junior Stewards, and the Tyler (doorkeeper). The latter is usually an elderly gentleman who may receive a few dollars for tending the door. The Secretary may also be a paid officer.

Before presenting the working of the degrees, we should explain that the ritual as presented in this chapter is that used in most American lodges. There may be trivial verbal variations, but no printed ritual could possibly conform to all the various rituals in use by the fifty-two Grand Lodges in this country. An analogy might be found in translations of the Lord's Prayer. One Christian body uses "which" and another "who art in heaven"; one uses "debts" and "debtors", and another "trespasses" and "those who trespass against us", while many add a doxology. Nevertheless, we know that we have the substance of the Our Father.

The reader should remember that his Masonic friends have taken an oath to conceal this ritual and will either refuse to discuss it altogether, change the subject, or simply deny its authenticity. Unless a Mason is well traveled and informed, he may honestly believe that since the work in his lodge differs slightly from that given in this chapter, this printed ritual is defective. If he has visited lodges in other states and has studied other rituals, he will know that minor differences exist in all of the fifty-two Grand Lodge rituals.

Three reasons account for the variations in rituals among the dozens of Masonic jurisdictions. First, there has never been a uniform ritual in England, the birthplace of the Craft, and therefore the American lodges inherited, not one, but several rituals. Second, until the beginning of the past century, English and American Masons considered it unessential to commit the ritual to memory in the word-for-word memorization that is now demanded. Third, the two rival English lodges, "Antients" and "Moderns", developed their own rituals and delivered these to their American counterparts. Masonic research workers can find predominantly Modern workings in Rhode Island, North Carolina, and Ohio and Antient workings in New York, New Jersey, and Michigan.

Each Grand Lodge employs a Grand Lecturer, who travels about the state giving instruction in the rituals and is supported by stipends from the lodges he visits. The material in this chapter has been gathered from decodings of the published *Ecce Orienti* (sometimes referred to as *King Solomon's*) books that are used by lodge officers. Each state has its own version, and the code employed can be broken by elementary cryptography. Two printed rituals, Ronayne's and Duncan's, are substantially accurate and often used by Masons themselves who do not wish to bother with the coded books. The details of the ritual are corroborated by Masonic Monitors, catalogues of paraphernalia, references in Masonic texts, and the testimony of seceders. The idea of genuine secrets in a mass organization of 2,100,000 men in the United States alone is preposterous, and we would not labor the point except that many seem to think that Masonry manages to keep its initiations and lodge rituals from those non-Masons who are interested in knowing them.

To keep this chapter within bounds, we have eliminated unnecessary repetitions and details that serve no purpose. A

Interior of a Masonic lodge, facing the Master's station.

verbatim account of the ritual and rubrics would comprise a small book in itself.

The interior of the lodge room features an altar in the center, on which rests the Volume of the Sacred Law, usually the Bible, and the square and compass. Nearby are three lighted tapers. The letter "G" is suspended or painted over the Master's chair and may be interpreted to stand for geometry or God.[1] The Master sits in the east and wears his apron, hat, sash, and jewel of office. Other members wear their white aprons and jewels of office if they are officeholders.

If candidates are to be inducted as Entered Apprentices, the Master calls the lodge to order in that degree. He begins,

---

[1] "The majority of masonic writers believe that the letter 'G' refers to Geometry, and the old catechisms also point that way": Bernard E. Jones, *Freemason's Guide and Compendium* (London: George G. Harrap, 1950), p. 299.

"I now declare this Lodge of Master Masons closed and Entered Apprentice in its stead. Brother Junior Deacon, inform the Tyler [the doorkeeper]; Brother Senior Deacon, attend at the altar [place both points of the compass under the square]." He raps once, and the members take their seats. He then instructs the Junior Deacon to take his assistants (Senior Steward and Junior Steward) to the anteroom where the candidate is waiting. The Secretary accompanies them to the anteroom and obtains affirmative answers to the following questions:

"Do you seriously declare, upon your honor, that, unbiased by friends, and uninfluenced by mercenary motives, you freely and voluntarily offer yourself as a candidate for the mysteries of Masonry?"

"Do you seriously declare, upon your honor, that you are prompted to solicit the privileges of Masonry by a favorable opinion of the institution, a desire for knowledge, and a sincere wish of being of service to your fellow creatures?"

"Do you seriously declare, upon your honor, that you will conform to all the ancient established usages of the Order?"

The Secretary returns to the lodge room and reports that the candidate has given the required answers. The candidate is now prepared for the first degree. He is instructed to remove his coat, shoes, stockings, and trousers and is divested of all metal articles: coins, watch, rings, and so on.[2] The Junior Deacon gives him a pair of trousers furnished by the lodge and asks him to put his left arm through the front of his shirt, exposing a bare arm and left breast. The Deacon

---

[2] "Freemasonry is essentially a Solar Cult and this prejudice against the use of m...ls [metals] in connection with religious observances is nearly always associated with the worship of the benign Spirits of Light": J. S. M. Ward, *The Masonic Why and Wherefore* (London: Baskerville Press, 1929), p. 1.

then puts a blindfold (called a hood-wink) on the candidate, places a slipper on his right foot, and loops a blue silk rope, called a cable tow, around his neck.

He leads the hoodwinked candidate to the lodge door and gives three knocks. The Senior Deacon inside reports, "Worshipful Master, there is an alarm at the inner door of our Lodge." The Master asks him to ascertain the cause of the alarm, and the Junior Deacon speaking for the Candidate responds, "Mr. ——, who has long been in darkness, and now seeks to be brought to light, and to receive a part in the rights and benefits of this worshipful Lodge, erected to God, and dedicated to the holy Sts. John, as all brothers and fellows have done before."[3]

(The dedication of the Lodge to the "Sts. John"—Saint John the Baptist and Saint John the Evangelist—is one of the few vestiges of Christianity found in contemporary Freemasonry.)

---

[3] "Without question Masonry demands of its adherent a denial of the Christian (and of every other so-called sectarian) religion. He must come as one in darkness, seeking light from the lodge, as one who is in spiritual ignorance, seeking wisdom. Since the lodge is nothing if not religious . . . it is religious light, religious wisdom, which is promised to its candidates. And by declaring that they are in darkness, the applicants formally, though not always consciously, reject the religious teachings of their Church as darkness. There is no escape from the conclusion that Masonry promises all of its members that they will find a higher, better religion in the lodge than is offered by the Christian Church": Theodore Graebner, *Is Masonry a Religion?* (St. Louis: Concordia Publishing House, 1946), p. 24.

In a series of questions put to the Junior Deacon, the Senior Deacon asks if the candidate is "worthy and well qualified", "duly and truly prepared", "of lawful age and properly vouched for", and "a man, free born, of good repute, and well recommended". The Senior Deacon closes the door, relays the answers to the Master, and takes the compass from the altar.

As the candidate and Junior Deacon enter the lodge room, the Senior Deacon presses one of the points of the compass to the candidate's bared left breast. "Mr. ——, on entering this Lodge for the first time, I receive you on the point of a sharp instrument pressing your naked left breast, which is to teach you, as this is an instrument of torture to your flesh, so should the recollection of it ever be to your mind and conscience, should you attempt to reveal the secrets of Masonry unlawfully." This ceremony is known as the "Shock of Entrance" or "Rite of Induction".

The Senior Deacon now takes over from the Junior Deacon and guides the candidate around the room. The Master interrupts, however, by asking, "Let no one enter on so important a duty without first involving the blessing of the Deity. Brother Senior Deacon, you will conduct the candidate to the center of the Lodge, and cause him to kneel for the benefit of prayer." The Master leaves his seat and kneels next to the candidate at the Masonic altar. They repeat the following prayer:

> Vouchsafe Thine aid, Almighty Father of the Universe, to this our present convention; and grant that this candidate for Masonry may dedicate and devote his life to Thy service, and become a true and faithful brother among us! Endue him with a competency of Thy divine wisdom, that, by the secrets of our art, he may be better enabled to display the beauties of brotherly love, relief, and truth, to the honor of Thy Holy Name. Amen.

All respond with the Masonic "So mote it be."

The Master rises, replaces his top hat, and takes the candidate by the right hand. "Mr. ———, in whom do you put your trust?" The candidate is prompted to answer, "In God." The Master comments, "Since in God you put your trust, your faith is well founded. Arise, follow your conductor, and fear no danger." The candidate is then led around the lodge, and the same questions put by the Senior Deacon earlier are repeated by the Junior Warden and Senior Warden. The Master also interrogates the candidate and continues, "From whence come you, and whither are you traveling?" The Senior Deacon answers for the candidate, "From the west, and traveling toward the east." Master: "Why leave you the west and travel toward the east?" Senior Deacon: "In search of light."

Master: "Since light is the object of your search, you will reconduct the candidate, and place him in charge of the Senior Warden in the west, with my orders that he teach this candidate to approach the east, the place of light, by advancing with one upright, regular step to the first stop, the heel of his right placed in the hollow of his left foot, his body erect at the altar before the Worshipful Master in the east."

The Senior Warden sees that the candidate has assumed the proper posture and tells the Master that he is ready. Again the Master leaves his seat and approaches the altar. "Mr. ———, you are now at the altar of Masonry for the first time; before you can be permitted to advance any further in Masonry, it becomes my duty to inform you, that you must take upon yourself a solemn oath or obligation, appertaining to this degree, which I, as Master of this Lodge, assure you will not materially interfere with the duty that you owe to your God, yourself, family, country, or neighbor. Are you willing to take such an oath?"

He replies that he is willing, and the Master continues, "Brother Senior Warden, you will place the candidate in due form, which is by kneeling on his naked left knee, his right forming the angle of a square, his left hand supporting the Holy Bible, square and compass, his right hand resting thereon. Mr. ——, you are now in position for taking upon yourself the solemn oath of an Entered Apprentice Mason, and, if you have no objections still, you will say I, and repeat your name after me.

I, ——, of my own free will and accord, in the presence of Almighty God, and this Worshipful Lodge, erected to Him, and dedicated to the holy Sts. John, do hereby and hereon [Master presses his gavel on candidate's knuckles] most solemnly and sincerely promise and swear, that I will always hail, ever conceal, and never reveal any of the arts, parts, or points of the hidden mysteries of Ancient Free Masonry, which may have been, or hereafter shall be, at this time, or any future period, communicated to me, as such, to any person or persons whomsoever, except it be to a true and lawful brother Mason, or in a regularly constituted Lodge of Masons; nor unto him or them until, by strict trial, due examination, or lawful information, I shall have found him, or them, as lawfully entitled to the same as I myself. I furthermore promise and swear that I will not print, paint, stamp, stain, cut, carve, mark or engrave them, or cause the same to be done, on any thing movable or immovable, capable of receiving the least impression of a word, syllable, letter, or character, whereby the same may become legible or intelligible to any person under the canopy of heaven, and the secrets of Masonry thereby unlawfully obtained through my unworthiness.

All this I most solemnly, sincerely promise and swear, with a firm and steadfast resolution to perform the same, without any mental reservation or secret evasion of mind whatever, binding myself under no less penalty than that of having my throat cut across, my tongue torn out by its roots, and my body buried in the rough sands of the sea, at low-water mark, where the tide ebbs and flows twice in twenty-four hours, should I ever knowingly violate this my Entered Apprentice obligation. So help me God, and keep me steadfast in the due performance of the same.

At the end of the oath the Master asks, "In token of your sincerity you will now detach your hands, and kiss the book on which your hands rest, which is the Holy Bible." The candidate complies, and the Master tells the Senior Deacon to release the cable tow, since "he is bound to us by an obligation—a tie stronger than lower hands can impose", and he is again asked what he most desires. He is prompted to say "Light." At this the Master says, "Brethren, you will stretch forth your hands, and assist me in bringing our newly made brother to light." The brethren surrounding the altar place their hands in the form of the Entered Apprentice due guard, and the Master quotes from Genesis, "In the beginning God created the heavens and the earth. And the earth was without form, and void; and darkness was upon the face of the waters. And God said, Let there be light, and there was light." At this the conductor jerks the blindfold from the candidate's eyes, and he sees the assembled lodge for the first time.

The Master now explains the light of Masonry.

My brother, on being brought to light in this degree, you discover both points of the compass hid by the square, which is to signify that you are yet in darkness as respects Masonry, you having only received the degree of an Entered Apprentice. You also discover the three great lights of Masonry, by the help of the three lesser. The three great lights in Masonry are the Holy Bible, square, and compass, which are thus explained: the Holy Bible is the rule and guide of our faith and practice; the square our actions; the compass, to circumscribe and keep us within bounds with all mankind, but more especially with a brother Mason. The three lesser lights are the three burning tapers which you see placed in a triangular form about this altar. They represent the sun, moon, and Master of the Lodge; and as the sun rules the day, and the moon governs the night, so ought the Worshipful Master to endeavor to rule and govern his Lodge with equal regularity.

Now the Master reveals the secret grip of this degree, which consists of pressing the thumb on the joint of the candidate's index finger. The Master and Senior Deacon then engage in a routine on the following order:

MASTER: What do you conceal?

Senior Deacon: All the secrets of Masons in Masonry to which this [here presses his thumb on the joint] token alludes.

MASTER: What is that?

S.D.: A grip.

MASTER: Of what?

S.D.: Of an Entered Apprentice Mason.

MASTER: Has it a name?

S.D.: It has.

MASTER: Will you give it me?

S.D.: I did not so receive it, neither will I so impart it.

MASTER: How will you dispose of it?

S.D.: I will letter and halve it with you.

MASTER: Letter and begin.

S.D.: No, you begin.

MASTER: You must begin.

S.D.: A.
MASTER: Z.
S.D.: Az.
MASTER: B.
S.D.: O.
MASTER: Bo.
S.D.: Boaz.

The candidate passes around the room, giving the due guard and sign of the Entered Apprentice at the various officers' stations. The Master presents a white lambskin apron to the candidate and says:

> Brother, I now present you with a lambskin or white apron, which is an emblem of innocence and the badge of a Mason, more ancient than the Golden Fleece or Roman Eagle, and, when worthily worn, more honorable than the Star and Garter, or any other order that can be conferred on you at this time, or any future period, by kings, princes, and potentates, or any other persons, except it be by Masons. I trust that you will wear it with equal pleasure to yourself and honor to the fraternity. You will carry it to the Senior Warden in the west, who will teach you how to wear it as an Entered Apprentice.

The Senior Warden ties it on the candidate with the flap turned up.

Now the Master addresses the candidate,

> Brother ——, agreeably to an ancient custom, adopted among Masons, it is necessary that you should be requested to deposit something of a metallic kind or nature, not for its intrinsic value, but that it may be laid up among the relics in the archives of this Lodge, as a memento that you were herein made a Mason. Anything, brother, that you may have about you will be thankfully received—a coin, a pin, anything.

Since the candidate was stripped of all his metallic possessions in the anteroom prior to entering the lodge, he has
nothing to contribute. His offer to get something from his
coat or trousers is refused, and he is usually somewhat embarrassed.

> Brother ——, you are indeed an object of charity—al-
> most naked, not one cent, not even a button or pin to
> bestow on this Lodge. Let this ever have, my brother, a
> lasting effect on your mind and conscience; and remem-
> ber, should you ever see a friend, but more especially a
> brother, in a like destitute condition, you will contribute
> as liberally to his support and relief as his necessities may
> seem to demand and your ability permit, without any
> material injury of yourself or family.

Now the candidate is allowed to return to the preparation
room and get dressed. He puts on his apron and returns to
the room, where the Master may take the occasion to deliver a sermon on the glories of the Craft and the meaning of
the working tools of the Entered Apprentice degree: the
twenty-four-inch gauge and the common gavel. The candidate is assigned to an older Mason who will instruct him in
the lecture of the degrees, a sort of catechism that the candidate must memorize prior to receiving the next degree and
repeat at a later meeting to a committee designated to test his
proficiency. It recapitulates the details of the ritual.

Finally, the Master delivers the Charge:

> As you are now introduced into the first principles of
> Masonry I congratulate you on being accepted into this
> ancient and honorable order; ancient, as having existed
> from time immemorial; and honorable, as tending in
> every particular so to render all men who will conform
> to its precepts. No human institution was ever raised on
> a better principle, or more solid foundation; nor were

| *Due guard of an Entered Apprentice* | *Sign of an Entered Apprentice* | *Due guard of a Fellow Craft Mason* | *Sign of a Fellow Craft Mason* |

ever more excellent rules and useful maxims laid down than are inculcated in the several Masonic lectures. The greatest and best of men in all ages have been encouragers and promoters of the art, and have never deemed it derogatory to their dignity to level themselves with the fraternity, extend their privileges, and patronize their assemblies.

There are three great duties, which, as a Mason, you are strictly to observe and inculcate—to God, your neighbor, and yourself. To God, in never mentioning His name but with the reverential awe which is due from a creature to his Creator: to implore His aid in all your laudable undertakings, and to esteem Him as your chief good. To your neighbor, in acting upon the square, and doing unto him as you would he should do unto you; and to yourself, in avoiding all irregularity and intemperance, which may impair your faculties or debase the dignity of your profession. A zealous attachment to these duties will insure public and private esteem.

Due guard of   Sign of   Grand hailing
a Master   a Master   sign of
Mason   Mason   distress

In the State you are to be a quiet and peaceable citizen, true to your government, and just to your country; you are not to countenance disloyalty or rebellion, but patiently submit to legal authority, and conform with cheerfulness to the government of the country in which you live.

In your outward demeanor be particularly careful to avoid censure or reproach. Let not interest, favor, or prejudice bias your integrity, or influence you to be guilty of a dishonorable action. And although your frequent appearance at our regular meetings is earnestly solicited, yet it is not meant that Masonry would interfere with your necessary avocations, for these are on no account to be neglected; neither are you to suffer your zeal for the institution to lead you into arguments with those who, through ignorance, may ridicule it. But, at your leisure hours, that you may improve in Masonic knowledge, you are to converse with well-informed brethren who will be always as ready to give as you will be ready to receive instruction.

Finally, keep sacred and inviolable the mysteries of the Order, as these are to distinguish you from the rest of the community, and mark your consequence among Masons. If, in the circle of your acquaintance, you find a person desirous of being initiated into Masonry, be particularly careful not to recommend him, unless you are convinced he will conform to our rules; that the honor, glory, and reputation of the institution may be firmly established, and the world at large convinced of its good effects.

The lodge is now closed, and the candidate will return on a later evening to take the second degree, that of Fellow Craft.

Many lodges find that few members bother to turn out for the working of this second degree. The curiosity about the new members is satisfied, and the substance of this degree is dull and commonplace.

The candidate is stripped of his clothing as in the preparation for the Entered Apprentice degree, but this time he slips his right arm out of his shirtsleeve, exposing his right arm and breast. The cable tow is wound twice around his arm, and the right foot and knee are bared. He is blindfolded, and a slipper is placed on his left foot. The Junior Deacon knocks on the lodge-room door and answers the Senior Deacon's inquiry with "Brother ———, who has been regularly initiated as Entered Apprentice, and now wishes to receive more light in Masonry by being passed to the degree of Fellow Craft." He answers a short series of questions regarding the candidate's proficiency in the first degree. The Junior Deacon whispers the password "Shibboleth" to the Senior Deacon, who closes the door, reports to the Master, and repeats the interrogations.

This time the Senior Deacon takes the square rather than the compass from the altar and, opening the door, says, "Let him enter and be received in due form." He places the angle of the square against the candidate's bare breast and declares, "Brother ———, on entering this Lodge the first time you were received on the points of a compass; I now receive you on the angle of the square, which is to teach you that the square of virtue should be the rule and guide of your conscience in all future transactions with mankind."

As the candidate is led twice around the lodge room, the Master reads a passage from the Old Testament: Amos 8:7–8. He is questioned by the Junior and Senior Wardens and the Master regarding his proficiency in the previous degree, and he tells the Master that he is in search of more light. Again the Master instructs the Senior Warden to teach the candidate the proper way to approach the east, this time by "two upright regular steps, his feet forming an angle of a square". He then places the candidate in position for taking his second oath. He kneels on his naked right knee before the altar, making his left knee form a square. His left arm from the shoulder to the elbow is held in a horizontal position with his forearm in a vertical position, forming a square. His right hand rests on an open Bible. The Master once more assures the candidate that nothing in the oath will interfere with any obligation to God, family, country, neighbor, or self. The oath follows.

I, ———, of my own free will and accord, in the presence of Almighty God, and this Worshipful Lodge, erected to Him and dedicated to the holy Sts. John, do hereby and hereon most solemnly and sincerely promise and swear that I will always hail, and ever conceal, and never reveal any of the secret arts, parts, or points of the Fellow Craft Degree to any person whomsoever, except it be to a true and lawful brother of this degree, or in a regularly constituted Lodge of Fellow Crafts; nor unto him or them until, by strict trial, due examination, or lawful information, I shall find him, or them, as lawfully entitled to the same as I am myself.

I furthermore promise and swear that I will stand to, and abide by, all the laws, rules, and regulations of the Fellow Craft Degree, as far as the same shall come to my knowledge.

Further, I will acknowledge and obey all due signs and summons sent to me from a Lodge of Fellow Crafts, or given me by a brother of that degree, if within the length of my cable-tow.

Further, that I will aid and assist all poor, distressed, worthy Fellow Crafts, knowing them to be such, as far as their necessities may require, and my ability permit, without any injury to myself.

Further, that I will not cheat, wrong, nor defraud a brother of this degree, knowingly, nor supplant him in any of his laudable undertakings.

All this I most solemnly promise and swear with a firm and steadfast resolution to perform the same, without any hesitation, mental reservation, or self-evasion of mind whatever, binding myself under no less penalty than of having my breast torn open, my heart plucked out, and placed on the highest pinnacle of the temple there to be devoured by the vultures of the air, should I ever knowingly violate the Fellow Craft obligation. So help me God, and keep me steadfast in the due performance of the same.

The ritual closely follows that of the first degree: the candidate asks for more light, the hoodwink is removed, the Master instructs him in the grip and password. The pass grip of a Fellow Craft is "Shibboleth", while the name of the real grip is "Jachin", which is given letter by letter. The candidate, speaking through the conductor, now relays this information on pass and grips to the Junior and Senior Wardens. The latter tucks a corner of the Masonic apron under the string, which is the manner in which Fellow Crafts must wear the emblem. The Master then explains the working tools of the degree: the plumb, square, and level.

Now the candidate is escorted out of the lodge room back to the anteroom, and the lodge room is rearranged for his second entry. Two large pillars about seven feet high are placed five feet apart near the door. Fifteen painted boards are arranged to represent three, five, and seven steps. The conductor addresses the candidate: "Brother ———, we are now about to make an ascent through a porch, by a flight of winding stairs, consisting of three, five, and seven steps, to a place representing the Middle Chamber of King Solomon's Temple, there to receive instructions relative to the wages due, and jewels of a Fellow Craft."

The conductor delivers a short commentary on operative and speculative Masonry. He reveals that the name of the left hand pillar is Boaz and that on the right, Jachin. They are supposed to represent the two pillars erected at the outer porch of King Solomon's Temple.

The first three steps have at least three meanings: the three principal stages of human life, namely, youth, manhood, and old age; also the "three principal supports in Masonry", Wisdom, Strength, and Beauty; and finally the three principal lodge officers, Master and Senior and Junior Wardens.

The five steps have two meanings: five orders of architecture (Tuscan, Doric, Ionic, Corinthian, and Composite) and five senses. The seven refer to all sorts of combinations: seven Sabbatical years, seven years building the temple, seven wonders of the world, seven planets, seven liberal arts and sciences.

Completing these fifteen steps, the Junior Warden asks the Senior Deacon to explain the pass "Shibboleth". He elaborates:

In consequence of a quarrel which long existed between Jephthah, judge of Israel, and the Ephraimites: the latter had been a stubborn rebellious people, whom Jephthah had endeavored to subdue by lenient measures, but to no effect. The Ephraimites, being highly incensed for not being called to fight and share in the rich spoils of the Ammonitish war, assembled a mighty army, and passed over the river Jordan to give Jephthah battle; but he, being apprised of their approach, called together the men of Gilead, and gave them battle, and put them to flight; and, to make his victory more complete, he ordered guards to be placed on the different passes on the banks of the river Jordan, and commanded, if the Ephraimites passed that way, Say ye Shibboleth; but they, being of a different tribe, could not frame to pronounce it aright, and pronounced it Sibboleth; which trifling defect proved them to be spies, and cost them their lives; and there fell at that time, at the different passes on the banks of the river Jordan, forty and two thousand. This word was also used by our ancient brethren to distinguish a friend from a foe, and has since been adopted as a password, to be given before entering every regulated and well-governed Lodge of Fellow Crafts.

Then the Senior Deacon asks for the real pass, "Jachin", and they pass to the Master, who delivers the following homily:

The first thing that particularly attracted your attention on your passage here was a representation of two brazen pillars, one on the left hand and the other on the right, which was explained to you by your conductor; after passing the pillars you passed a flight of winding stairs, consisting of three, five, and seven steps, which was likewise explained to you; after passing the stairs, you arrived at the outer door of the Middle Chamber, which you found closely guarded by the Junior Warden, who demanded of you the pass and token of the pass of a Fellow Craft; you next arrived at the inner door of the Middle Chamber, which you found guarded by the Senior Warden, who demanded of you the grip and word of a Fellow Craft. You have now arrived at the Middle Chamber, where you are received and recorded a Fellow Craft. You are now entitled to wages, as such; which are, the Corn of nourishment, the Wine of refreshment, and the Oil of joy, which donate peace, harmony, and strength. You are also entitled to the jewels of Fellow Craft; which are, an attentive ear, an instructive tongue, and faithful breast. The attentive ear receives the sound from the instructive tongue, and the mysteries of Masonry are safely lodged in the repository of faithful breasts.

He concludes with the charge, and the candidate is left to memorize the lecture, which rehashes the degree work.

At last the Masonic candidate is ready for the concluding degree, the third. As many as three candidates for the third degree will be inducted in one evening. All will go through the first section of the work together, but then each candidate must complete the degree in a separate ceremony, which lasts from an hour to an hour and a half. A medium-sized lodge that enrolls perhaps thirty new members a year will thus have to schedule at least ten Master Mason initiations.

This degree, built around the legend of the assassination of Hiram Abiff, the builder of King Solomon's Temple, sometimes takes up to two hours for its full performance. Nowhere in the Bible do we read anything about Hiram's tragic death; only Masonic myth fills in the details of his demise. During the conferring of this degree the lodge is known as the "Sanctum Sanctorum of King Solomon's Temple".

This time the candidate rolls up his trousers on both legs and takes both arms out of his shirt, leaving legs and breast bare. The silk cable tow is wrapped around his waist three times and he is blindfolded. He gains entry into the lodge room by answering the usual questions through his spokesman, the Junior Deacon, and gives the password, "Tubal Cain".

The Senior Deacon stops him at the door:

Brother ———, on entering this Lodge the first time, you were received on the point of the compass, pressing your naked left breast, the moral of which was explained to you. On entering the second time, you were received on the angle of the square, which was also explained to you. I now receive you on both points of the compass, extending from your naked left to your naked right breast, which is to teach you that as the vital parts of man are contained within the breast, so the most excellent tenets of our institution are contained between the points of the compass—which are Friendship, Morality, and Brotherly Love.

The Senior Deacon escorts the third-degree candidate around the lodge room three times while the Master recites a passage from the Bible. Sometimes in larger lodges a musical paraphrase will be sung and accompanied on the organ. He is instructed by the Senior Warden to place his feet, heels touching and toes pointed outward. The Master then asks that the candidate kneel at the altar with both hands on the Volume of the Sacred Law, square, and compass. The Master Mason's oath follows:

I, ———, of my own free will and accord, in the presence of Almighty God, and this Worshipful Lodge, erected to Him and dedicated to the holy Sts. John, do hereby and hereon most solemnly and sincerely promise and swear,

Candidate takes the oath of a Master Mason.

that I will always hail, ever conceal, and never reveal any of the secrets, arts, parts, point or points, of the Master Masons' Degree, to any person or persons whomsoever, except that it be to a true and lawful brother of this Degree, or in a regularly constituted Lodge of Master Masons, nor unto him, or them, until by strict trial, due examination, or lawful information, I shall have found him, or them, as lawfully entitled to the same as I am myself.

I furthermore promise and swear, that I will stand to and abide by all laws, rules, and regulations of the Master Mason's Degree, and of the Lodge of which I may hereafter become a member, as far as the same shall come to my knowledge; and that I will ever maintain and support the constitution, laws, and edicts of the Grand Lodge under which the same shall be holden.

Further, that I will acknowledge and obey all due signs and summonses sent to me from a Master Mason's Lodge, or given me by a brother of that Degree, if within the length of my cable tow.

Further, that I will always aid and assist all poor, distressed, worthy Master Masons, their widows and orphans, knowing them to be such, as far as their necessities may require, and my ability permit, without material injury to myself and family.

Further, that I will keep a worthy brother Master Mason's secrets inviolable, when communicated to and received by me as such, murder and treason excepted.

Further, that I will not aid, nor be present at, the initiation, passing, or raising of a woman, an old man in his dotage, a young man in his nonage, an atheist, a madman, or fool, knowing them to be such.

Further, that I will not sit in a Lodge of clandestine-made Masons, nor converse on the subject of Masonry with a clandestine-made Mason, nor one who has been expelled or suspended from a Lodge, while under the sentence, knowing him or them to be such.

Further, I will not cheat, wrong, nor defraud a Master Mason's Lodge, nor a brother of this Degree, knowingly, nor supplant him in any of his laudable undertakings, but will give him due and timely notice, that he may ward off all danger.

Further, that I will not knowingly strike a brother Master Mason, or otherwise do him personal violence in anger, except in the necessary defence of my family or property.

Further, that I will not have illegal carnal intercourse with a Master Mason's wife, his mother, sister, or daughter knowing them to be such, nor suffer the same to be done by others, if in my power to prevent.

Further, that I will not give the Grand Masonic word, in any other manner or form than that in which I shall receive it, and then in a low breath.

Further, that I will not give the Grand Hailing Sign of Distress except in case of the most imminent danger, in a just and lawful Lodge, or for the benefit of instruction; and if ever I should see it given, or hear the words accompanying it, by a worthy brother in distress, I will fly to his relief, if there is a greater probability of saving his life than losing my own.

All this I most solemnly, sincerely promise and swear, with a firm and steady resolution to perform the same, without any hesitation, mental reservation, or secret evasion of mind whatever, binding myself, under no less penalty than that of having my body severed in two, my bowels taken from thence and burned to ashes, the ashes scattered before the four winds of heaven, that no more remembrance might be had of so vile and wicked a wretch as I would be, should I ever, knowingly, violate this my Master Mason's obligation. So help me God, and keep me steadfast in the due performance of the same.

The usual routine of asking for further light and removing the hoodwink follows the administration of the oath. He is shown how to wear the apron of a full-fledged Mason and is told about the use of the trowel, the main third-degree working tool. The Master tells the candidate he may retire to the anteroom while the lodge takes thirty minutes of refreshment, a Masonic term for recreation.

Unless forewarned, the candidate may expect that nothing more remains but the usual platitudes in the charge. As a matter of fact, the work on his final degree is just beginning. The altar, lights, and pillars are removed, and some of the brethren fetch the paraphernalia used in the completion of the ceremony.

The candidate returns to the lodge room to receive the congratulations of the other members. They ask him how he enjoyed the work and if he is not glad it is through. The

Master calls the lodge to "labor" and asks the Senior Warden, Junior Warden, and Secretary if they have any further business for the evening. They reply in the negative, but the Master calls the candidate to his seat in the east. "Brother ———, I presume you now consider yourself a Master Mason, and, as such, entitled to all the privileges of a Master Mason, do you not?" He replies that he does.

> Brother ———, you are not yet a Master Mason, neither do I know that you ever will be, until I know how well you will withstand the amazing trials and dangers that await you. The Wardens and brethren of this Lodge require a more satisfactory proof of your fidelity to your trust, before they are willing to intrust you with the more valuable secrets of this Degree. You have a rough and rugged road to travel, beset with thieves, robbers, and murderers; and should you lose your life in the attempt, it will not be the first instance of the kind, my brother. You will remember in whom you put your trust, with that divine assurance, that "he who endureth unto the end, the same shall be saved." Heretofore you have had some one to pray for you, but now you have none. You must pray for yourself. You will therefore suffer yourself to be again hoodwinked, and kneel where you are, and pray orally or mentally, as you please. When through, signify by saying Amen, and arise and pursue your journey.

At this point the Junior Warden assumes the role of Jubela, the first ruffian, and grasps the blindfolded candidate by the collar. A dialogue follows.

RUFFIAN: Grand Master Hiram Abiff, I am glad to meet you thus alone. I have long sought this opportunity. You will remember you promised us, that when the Temple was completed, we should receive the secrets of a Master Mason, whereby we might travel in foreign countries, work, and receive Master's wages. Behold! the Temple is now about to be completed, and we have not obtained that which we have so long sought. At first, I did not doubt your veracity; but now I do! I therefore now demand of you the secrets of a Master Mason!

CONDUCTOR (for candidate): Brother, this is an unusual way of asking for them. It is neither a proper time nor place; but be true to your engagement, and I will be true to mine. Wait until the Temple is completed, and then, if you are found worthy and well qualified, you will unquestionably receive the secrets of a Master Mason; but, until then, you cannot.

RUFFIAN: This does not satisfy me! Talk not to me of time or place, but give me the secrets of a Master Mason, or I will take your life!

CONDUCTOR: I cannot; nor can they be given, except in the presence of Solomon, king of Israel, Hiram, king of Tyre, and myself.

RUFFIAN: That does not satisfy me. I'll hear no more of your cavilling! Give me the Master's word, or I will take your life in a moment!

Jubela brushes the candidate's throat with his hand and steps aside so that the conductor may shuffle the candidate along to the Senior Warden's station. The Senior Warden, playing the part of Jubelo, also seizes the candidate's collar and demands the secrets of a Master Mason. He brushes the left breast of the candidate, who is hustled along to the Master's seat. The Master takes both collars of the candidate's coat while shouting, "You have escaped Jubela and Jubelo—me you cannot escape. My name is Jubelum. What I purpose, I perform. I hold in my hand an instrument of death; therefore, give me the secrets of a Master Mason, or I will take your life instantly!" The conductor answers for the

*Jubelum taps the candidate with a setting maul
as members of the lodge wait to catch him in canvas.*

jostled candidate, "I will not." Jubelum declares, "Then die!"

At this Jubelum hits the candidate a light blow on the head with a stuffed setting maul, pushes him backward and trips him so that he falls into a seven-foot-by-six-foot canvas held by several of the brethren. He is lowered to the floor, bewildered and perhaps frightened. Remember that he is blindfolded.

Jubelum asks if he is dead, and the brethren reply, "He is; his skull is broken in." Jubelum: "What horrid deed is this we have done? Brethren: We have murdered our Grand Master, Hiram Abiff, and have not obtained that which we have sought; this is not the time for vain reflection—the question is, what shall we do with the body?" They decide to bury it in the rubbish of the Temple until low twelve, when they plan to meet and give it a decent burial. The lodge becomes silent until the Master strikes the hour of low twelve (midnight) on a triangle or bell. The three ruffians appear to carry out the burial, and a group of brethren hoist the canvas-wrapped body of the candidate onto their shoulders and carry it around the lodge three times. They pretend to bury it and plant an acacia plant at the head in order to identify the spot. The conspirators plot to escape but are unable to deliver the pass needed to board a ship to Ethiopia; they decide to flee to the interior.

Now the remaining brethren begin to shout, laugh, and move about. They are supposed to be Temple workmen who report to the Master (who now plays King Solomon) that no work has been laid out on the trestle board and that they therefore have no work to do. A search is undertaken for Hiram, and a roll call taken of the Fellow Crafts. They soon discover that the three assassins are absent. Meanwhile, twelve Fellow Crafts are admitted to King Solomon's presence, kneel before him, and confess that they and the three murderers entered into a conspiracy to extort the secrets of a Master Mason from Hiram, but they backed out. The King deputizes them to find the three escapees. Three of them sit down near the candidate, discover the newly planted acacia, and hear the assassins accusing themselves of their crime. They overpower the ruffians and drag them to Solomon, to whom they admit their guilt.

> Vile, impious wretches! despicable villains! reflect with horror on the atrocity of your crime, and on the amiable character of your Worshipful Grand Master, whom you have so basely assassinated. Hold up your heads, and hear your sentence. It is my orders that you be taken without the gates of the court, and be executed, according to your several imprecations, in the clefts of the rocks. Brother

Junior Grand Warden, you will see my orders duly executed. Begone!

The brethren rush into the anteroom and set up a clamor amid the groans of the "dying" ruffians. They return to tell Solomon that they have carried out the execution, and he further orders them, "You twelve Fellow Crafts will go in search of the body, and, if found, observe whether the Master's word, or a key to it, or anything that appertains to the Master Degree, is on or about it."

They stroll over to where the candidate lies shrouded in the canvas and discover the grave.

> Here is the body of our Grand Master, Hiram Abiff, in a mangled and putrid state. Let us go and report. But what were our orders? We were ordered to observe whether the Master's word, or a key to it, or anything appertaining to the Master's Degree was on or about the body; but, brothers, we are only Fellow Crafts, and know nothing about the Master's word, or a key to it, or anything appertaining to the Master's Degree; we must, however, make an examination, or we will be put to death.

They fumble around the candidate's body and find the jewel that was attached to the yoke around his neck. "This is the jewel of his office", they exclaim, and they detach the jewel and take it to King Solomon. They inform Solomon that they have been unable to find the Master's word, and he tells the Treasurer: "My worthy brother of Tyre, as the Master's word is now lost, the first sign given at the grave and the first word spoken, after the body is raised, shall be adopted for the regulation of all Master's lodges, until future generations shall find out the right." By this the lodge hints at the discovery of the true Master's word, which is given in the Royal Arch degree for those who wish to advance through the York rite.

All now form a circle around the body and sing the Masonic funeral dirge, which is also used in Masonic burial services.

At the conclusion of the hymn the Master makes the grand hailing sign of distress by throwing both arms in the air. He exclaims, "O Lord my God, I fear the Master's word is lost forever." He tells the Junior Warden, "You will take the body by the Entered Apprentice grip, and see if it can be raised." He halfheartedly grasps the candidate's hand but lets it slip out. "Most Worshipful King Solomon, owing to the high state of putrefaction, it having been dead already fifteen days, the skin slips, and the body cannot be raised", he relates. The Master repeats the grand hailing sign and ejaculation and asks the Senior Warden to try raising the body with the Fellow Craft's grip. He too reports, "Owing to the reason given before, the flesh cleaves from the bone, and the body cannot be so raised." The Master wails, "O Lord my God; O Lord my God! O Lord my God! Is there no hope for the widow's son?" All kneel and repeat the following prayer:

Thou, O God! knowest our down-sitting and our uprising, and understandest our thoughts afar off. Shield and defend us from the evil intentions of our enemies, and support us under the trials and afflictions we are destined to endure, while traveling through this vale of tears. Man that is born of a woman is of few days and full of trouble. He cometh forth as a flower, and is cut down: he fleeth also as a shadow, and continueth not. Seeing his days are determined, the number of his months are with thee; thou hast appointed his bounds that he cannot pass, turn from him that he may rest, till he shall accomplish his day. For there is hope a tender branch thereof will not cease. But man dieth and wasteth away; yea, man giveth up the ghost, and where is he? As the waters fail from the sea, and the flood decayeth and drieth up, so man lieth down, and riseth not up till the heavens shall be no more. Yet, O Lord! have compassion on the children of thy creation, administer and comfort in time of trouble, and save them with an everlasting salvation. Amen.

Finally the Master sighs, "My worthy brother of Tyre, I shall endeavor to raise the body by the strong grip, or lion's paw, of the tribe of Judah." He grips the candidate with the Master Mason's grip and pulls him to his feet, giving him the grand Masonic word on the five points of fellowship. The word is "Ma-hah-bone", which the Master whispers to the candidate and asks him to repeat with him. The two exchange this word on the so-called five points of fellowship: foot to foot, knee to knee, breast to breast, hand to back, and cheek to cheek or mouth to ear. The candidate's blindfold has been slipped off, and he sees light for the first time in about an hour. The following explanation of the five points is given by the Master:

> First: Foot to foot—that you will never hesitate to go on foot, and out of your way, to assist and serve a worthy brother.
> Second: Knee to knee—that you will ever remember a brother's welfare, as well as your own, in all your adorations to Deity.
> Third: Breast to breast—that you will ever keep in your breast a brother's secrets, when communicated to and received by you as such, murder and treason excepted.
> Fourth: Hand to back—that you will ever be ready to stretch forth your hand to assist and save a fallen brother; and that you will vindicate his character behind his back, as well as before his face.

The five points of fellowship.

Fifth: Cheek to cheek, or mouth to ear—that you will ever caution and whisper good counsel in the ear of an erring brother and, in the most friendly manner, remind him of his errors and aid his reformation, giving him due and timely notice, that he may ward off approaching danger.

All the brethren take their seats while the candidate stands before the Master in the east and hears a lecture on the degree. This recounts the parts of the degree and the Hiram Abiff legend. He concludes by explaining the three grand Masonic pillars:

The pillar of Wisdom represents Solomon, King of Israel, whose wisdom contrived the mighty fabric; the pillar of Strength, Hiram, King of Tyre, who strengthened Solomon in his grand undertaking; the pillar of Beauty, Hiram Abiff, the widow's son, whose cunning craft and curious workmanship beautified and adorned the Temple.

The construction of this grand edifice was attended with two remarkable circumstances. From Josephus we learn, that although seven years were occupied in building it, yet, during the whole time, it rained not in the daytime, that the workmen might not be obstructed in their labor, and from sacred history it appears that there was neither the sound of hammer, nor axe, nor any tool of iron, heard in the house while it was building. This famous fabric was supported by fourteen hundred and fifty-three columns, and two thousand nine hundred and six pilasters—all hewn from the finest Parian marble.

There were employed in its building three Grand Masters; three thousand three hundred Masters, or overseers of the work; eighty thousand Fellow Crafts, or hewers on the mountains and in the quarries; and seventy thousand Entered Apprentices, or bearers of burdens. All these were classes and arranged in such a manner, by the wisdom of Solomon, that neither envy, discord, nor confusion was suffered to interrupt that universal peace and tranquillity which pervaded the world at that important period.

Brother ——, seven constitute a Lodge of Entered Apprentices—one Master Mason, and six Entered Apprentices. They usually meet on the Ground Floor of King Solomon's Temple.

Five constitute a Lodge of Fellow Crafts—two Master Masons and three Fellow Crafts. They usually meet in the Middle Chamber of King Solomon's Temple.

Three constitute a Lodge of Master Masons—three Master Masons. They meet in the Sanctum Sanctorum, or Holy of Holies of King Solomon's Temple.

He also explains more Masonic symbols, such as the three steps, the pot of incense, beehive, book of constitutions, sword pointing to a naked heart, the all-seeing eye, the anchor and ark and the forty-seventh problem of Euclid, the hourglass, scythe, setting maul, coffin, grave, acacia, and spade.

The Master delivers a charge to the lodge, which follows:

And now, my brethren, let us see to it, and so regulate our lives by the plumb-line of justice, ever squaring our actions by the square of virtue, that when the Grand Warden of Heaven may call for us, we may be found ready; let us cultivate assiduously the noble tenets of our profession—brotherly love, relief, and truth—and, from the square, learn morality; from the level, equality; from the plumb, rectitude of life. Let us imitate, in all his various perfections, him who, when assailed by the murderous band of rebellious craftsmen, maintained his integrity, even in death, and sealed his pledge with his own blood. Let us emulate his amiable and virtuous conduct, his unfeigned piety to his God, his inflexible integrity to his trust; and as the evergreen that bloomed at the head of the grave betoken the place of his interment, so may virtue's ever-blooming loveliness designate us as free and accepted Masons. With the trowel, spread liberally the cement of brotherly love and affection; and, circumscribed by the compass, let us ponder well our words and actions, and let all the energies of our minds and the affections of our souls be employed in the attainment of our Supreme Grand Warden's approbation. Thus, when dissolution draws nigh, and the cold winds of death come sighing around us, and his chilly dews already glisten on our foreheads, with joy shall we obey the summons of the Grand Warden of Heaven, and go from our labors on earth to everlasting refreshments in the Paradise of God. Then, by the benefit of the pass—a pure and blameless life—with a firm reliance on Divine Providence, shall we gain ready admission into that Celestial Lodge above, where the Supreme Grand Warden forever presides—forever reigns. When, placed at his right hand, he will be pleased to pronounce us just and upright Masons, then shall we be fitted as living stones for that spiritual temple, "that house not made with hands, eternal in the heavens," where no discordant voice shall be heard, but all the soul shall experience shall be perfect bliss, and all it shall express shall be perfect praise, and love divine shall ennoble every heart, and hallelujahs exalted employ every tongue.

The degree work concludes with the following charge to the newly made Master Mason:

Brother, your zeal for the institution of Masonry, the progress you have made in the mystery, and your conformity to our regulations, have pointed you out as a proper object for our favor and esteem.

You are now bound by duty, honor, and gratitude, to be faithful to your trust; to support the dignity of your character on every occasion; and to enforce, by precept and example, obedience to the tenets of the Order.

In the character of a Master Mason, you are authorized to correct the errors and irregularities of your uninformed brethren, and to guard them against a breach of fidelity.

To preserve the reputation of the fraternity unsullied must be your constant care; and, for this purpose, it is your province to recommend to your inferiors obedience and submission; to your equals, courtesy and affability; to your superiors, kindness and condescension. Universal benevolence you are always to cultivate; and, by the regularity of your own behavior, afford the best example for the conduct of others less informed. The ancient landmarks of the order, intrusted to your care, you are carefully to preserve; and never suffer them to be infringed, or countenance a deviation from the established usages and customs of the fraternity.

Your virtue, honor, and reputation are concerned in supporting with dignity the character you now bear. Let no motive, therefore, make you swerve from your duty, violate your vows, or betray your trust; but be true and faithful, and imitate the example of that celebrated artist whom you this evening represent. Thus you will render yourself deserving of the honor which we have conferred, and merit the confidence we have reposed.

As usual, there is a catechism or lecture that the candidate must commit to memory and recite at a later meeting. The candidate is now in possession of all Masonic secrets, whose disclosure he has sworn to protect by a solemn oath.

The monotony of these three degrees drives many older members to discontinue attending the lodge on any regular basis or to enter the Scottish and York rites in search of a greater variety and newer experience in Masonry.

CHAPTER IV

SCOTTISH AND YORK RITES

Master Masons Attend Graduate School

Most Masons go no farther than the Blue Lodge, but about one out of three elects to advance through either or both of the two principal systems of "higher degrees". Neither the Scottish rite nor the York rite constitutes an integral part of the Masonic order and neither is officially recognized by the Grand Lodges.

Claims of these two rites to form a part of Freemasonry rest only on the requirement that their initiates must be Master Masons. Expulsion from the so-called "higher degrees" or appendant bodies does not affect Blue Lodge membership. On the other hand, a Mason expelled from the Craft degrees is automatically excluded from the dependent "higher degrees". Therefore, membership in these higher degrees demands maintenance of membership in a Blue Lodge. Relations between the Blue Lodges and these rites are friendly, but a high-ranking Scottish-rite Mason or a Knight Templar exercises no precedence in local Blue Lodges, nor may he wear his jewels of office or insignia of the rites in the lodge.

In theory and in fact, the individual state Grand Lodges are far more powerful than the Scottish rite. A Grand Master "outranks" any 33rd-degree Mason. Of course, most state officers are also involved in the Scottish or York rites. Still, the Blue Lodge of three degrees is the basic unit of Masonry, just as the parish is the basic unit of parochial organization, and the Grand Lodge of each state is the Masonic "diocese".

Bernard E. Jones, author of the most reliable history of English Masonry, writes:

> The additional degrees are often called the "higher degrees," but the term seems hardly fair to "pure, ancient masonry." The "highest" degrees must always remain those which authentic masonic history proves to be the oldest. They are the three Craft degrees. Other degrees may be designated by higher numbers but in no sense other than, in some cases, that of a more highly developed symbolism, can they be said to be higher—a statement which does not in any way detract from their value or beauty. The Grand Lodges of England and of all English-speaking countries acknowledge the Craft degrees and, to a varying extent, Royal Arch masonry and Mark masonry. All other degrees are "additional" or "side" degrees, and among them the Rose Croix and the Knights Templar occupy honoured and exceptional places.[1]

Nevertheless, hundreds of thousands of Masons who are interested in acquiring the added prestige of the "higher degrees" and who are financially able to do so continue in one or both of the two rites. A Master Mason who wishes to become a 32nd-degree Mason must pay an initiation fee of at least $175 and spend several days going through the ceremonies at a Scottish-rite cathedral. Those who choose to climb the ladder of the York, or, as it is sometimes known, the American rite, take a series of degrees before becoming Knights Templar.

[1] Bernard E. Jones, *Freemason's Guide and Compendium* (London: George G. Harrap, 1950), p. 549.

Some Masonic purists complain that many of their brethren enter the rites only to qualify for membership in the Shrine. Master Masons are repeatedly urged to take the "higher degrees". Louis B. Blakemore, president of the Masonic History Co., explains why many Blue Lodge Masons are induced to enter the rites:

> After taking his Third Degree the neophyte emerges considerably dazed in more ways than one. He then begins to wonder exactly what it means and what it is all about. At this point he is usually told that if he will just take the further or so called "higher" degrees all will be made clear to him, but neither the miscalled Scottish or York Rite ever throws, or even attempts to throw, much light upon the meaning of Symbolic Masonry.

Once Masonry was transplanted across the English Channel, the French devotees set about devising literally hundreds of higher degrees. The manufacture and sale of spurious Masonic degrees proved profitable, and the proprietors of various rites sought to control French Masonry by inventing higher and higher degrees. The surviving Scottish and York rites are only the two most successful of the dozens of rites that have sprung up. The ninety-six-degree Rite of Memphis, composed in France in 1814, is now extinct, but a few exotic rites still claim followings, especially in the Grand Orients.

The thirty-three–degree system of the Ancient and Accepted Scottish Rite is built on the Rite of Perfection of twenty-five degrees devised in the Chapter of Clermont in 1754. Some of the original degrees are said to have been composed by the Chevalier Ramsay, a Scottish Presbyterian turned Catholic, who attempted to use the new Masonic order to restore the Stuarts to the English throne.

In 1758 a body styling itself the *Conseils des Empereurs d'Orient et d'Occident*, whose members were known as

Sovereign Masonic Princes, began to issue charters to work this Rite of Perfection. Three years later Stephen Morin, reportedly a Jew, was commissioned to propagate this rite in the Americas. He set up shop in Santo Domingo, West Indies, and conferred the degrees on Moses M. Hayes, who appointed Isaac Da Costa as Deputy Inspector General for South Carolina. Within five years, Morin was charged with "propagating strange and monstrous doctrines", and his charter was withdrawn. He disappeared from the scene.

The Grand Lodge of Perfection was established at Charleston, S.C., in 1783 and became the Supreme Council in 1801. John Mitchell and the Rev. Frederick Dalcho, an Episcopal clergyman, headed this new Council. Four Jews and three Christians completed the Council's roster. Although the English branch of the Ancient and Accepted Rite is closed to non-Christians, the parent Supreme Council has never set up a Christian qualification for admittance.

Eight degrees imported from Europe were added to the reshuffled twenty-five degrees of the Rite of Perfection in 1802. In order to justify this action the legend was planted that a thirty-three-degree system had been authorized by Frederick the Great of Prussia, who became the posthumous patron of the rite. Frederick had dabbled in Masonry at one time but had soon lost interest in the lodge and had died in 1786. The patriarch of the Scottish rite, Albert Pike, admits, "There is no doubt that Frederick came to the conclusion that the great pretensions of Masonry in the blue degrees were merely imaginary and deceptive. He ridiculed the Order and thought its ceremonies mere child's play; and some of his sayings to that effect have been preserved." No Masonic historian now regards the part played by Frederick in the formation of the Scottish rite as anything but mythical. The kindest word that may be said for those who perpetrated this hoax is that they considered such a fraud essential to entice Masons to purchase their degrees.

A Northern Jurisdiction, which covers states north of the Ohio and east of the Mississippi Rivers, began to function in 1813 and now maintains headquarters in Lexington, Massachusetts, while the Southern Jurisdiction has moved from Charleston to Washington, D.C. The latter embraces thirty-seven southern and western states, including Minnesota, Iowa, and North Dakota. The northern branch claims 345,000 members in fifteen other states. Membership in the Southern Jurisdiction has declined from 651,899 in 1979 to 495,000 in 1997. The Southern Jurisdiction supports children's hospitals in Atlanta and Dallas as well as forty clinics that treat childhood language disorders.

Pike must be credited with bringing the Scottish rite to the position of prestige it occupies today. It is said that he found Masonry in a log cabin and left it in a temple. A teacher-trapper-journalist-lawyer-poet-Confederate general, Pike busied himself in the fields of esoteric Masonry and oriental religion. Regarding esoteric Masonry, he had the field pretty much to himself, since few men of learning would bother with the fables and pretensions of the Craft. Religiously, Pike was more of an occultist and pagan than a Christian, and his personal philosophy was woven into his revisions of the Scottish-rite rituals, especially those of the Southern Jurisdiction, which he served as Grand Commander for thirty-two years from 1859. His *Morals and Dogma*, a turgid 861-page commentary on the thirty-three degrees, is still the standard monitor, and copies are often presented to new members.

Pike seemed to challenge the adequacy of Blue Lodge Masonry when he wrote:

The Blue Degrees are but the outer court or portico of the Temple. Part of the symbols are displayed there to the Initiate, but he is intentionally misled by false interpretations. It is not intended that he shall understand them; but it is intended that he shall imagine he understands them. Their true explication is reserved for the Adepts, the Princes of Masonry. . . . It is well enough for the mass of those called Masons, to imagine that all is contained in the Blue Degrees; and whoso attempts to undeceive them will labor in vain and without true reward violate his obligation as an Adept.[2]

We must realize, of course, that Pike was selling his particular brand of "higher" Masonry, although his patronizing attitude toward other Masons and his frank admissions of deceit and false interpretations must annoy many brethren. He had to dangle a carrot before Masons who were quite satisfied to remain in Craft Masonry.

While the York rite, culminating in the Knights Templar degree, refuses admission to any but Christian Masons, the Scottish rite in the United States repudiates any specifically Christian qualification.

All the Degrees of Scottish Masonry can be received by good men of every race and religious faith; and any Degree that cannot be so received is not Masonry, which is universal, but some other thing that is exclusive and therefore intolerant. All our degrees have, in that, one object. Each inculcates toleration, and the union of men of all faiths; and each erects a platform on which the Mohammedan, the Israelite, and the Christian may stand side by side and hand in hand, as true brethren.[3]

[2] Albert Pike, *Morals and Dogma* (Charleston, S.C.: Supreme Council of the Thirty-third Degree for the Southern Jurisdiction of the United States, 1881), p. 819.

[3] *Liturgy of the Ancient and Accepted Scottish Rite of Freemasonry for the Southern Jurisdiction of the U.S.A.* (1936), part 3, p. 173.

Various elaborations on the King Solomon's Temple theme and certain occult material are illustrated in the Scottish-rite degrees. Mackey states, "Some of these legends have concurrent support of Scripture; some are related by Josephus; and some appear to have no historical foundation." Several of the degrees describe the vengeance wreaked on the assassins of Hiram Abiff: Jubela, Jubelo, and Jubelum.

Since the working of the Scottish-rite degrees demands elaborate props, costumes, scenery, furniture, and trapdoors, the Scottish-rite cathedrals are found only in the larger cities and draw on a membership in a large radius. Several hundred men may advance from Master Mason to 32nd degree in ceremonies that typically take a weekend to complete. Sometimes these degrees are conferred in a class that meets weekly over a period of several months. Most of the initiates watch the proceedings from the sidelines while small groups of a dozen men may go through a particular degree as representatives of the entire class.

Not all the twenty-nine degrees are worked in any particular initiation, but the essence of those skipped over is communicated to the candidates. An introduction to the Northern Jurisdiction assures prospective members: "A candidate is not required to commit the Scottish Rite degrees, signs, passwords, tokens or grips to memory. No examinations are given either during the degree work nor for admission to the meetings of other Valleys [Scottish-rite centers]."[4]

In England the Ancient and Accepted Rite was introduced from America in 1846 but dropped the title "Scottish" in 1909. Only Christians may take the 18th, or Rose Croix, degree, and therefore all 32nd- and 33rd-degree Masons in that country are Christians. The English rite works

[4] *The Facts of Scottish Rite* (Boston: Supreme Council 33, Ancient Accepted Scottish Rite, Northern Masonic Jurisdiction, U.S.A., 1963), p. 15.

only the 18th, 30th, 31st, and 32nd degrees, the others being conferred titularly. The English rite limits the number of 31st-degree Masons to 600, 32nd to 250, and 33rd to 70, plus eight honorary 33rds.

Both the Scottish and York rites have waived the right to confer the basic three degrees. The Blue Lodges would certainly not appreciate any encroachment on these grounds. In the Northern Jurisdiction of the Scottish rite, the 4th to 14th degrees are conferred in a Lodge of Perfection. The next two degrees are conferred in a Council Princes of Jerusalem. A Chapter of Rose Croix controls the 17th and 18th degrees. Finally, a Consistory controls the 19th through 32nd degrees. The 33rd degree is bestowed on a limited number of 32nd-degree Masons each year who have distinguished themselves as Masons.

Dozens of oaths are administered in progressing through the series of Scottish-rite degrees. A sample oath would be that of the 10th degree, Master Elect of Fifteen:

I, ———, do promise and swear upon the Holy Bible, never to reveal where I have received this degree, nor even say who assisted at my reception, and I furthermore promise never to receive any in this degree without a full power from my superiors. Nor to assist at any reception unless in a regular manner and Chapter of this degree. To keep exactly in my heart all the secrets that shall be revealed to me. And in failure of this, my obligation, I consent to have my body opened perpendicularly, and to be exposed for eight hours in the open air, that the venomous flies may eat my entrails, my head to be cut off and put on the highest pinnacle of the world, and I will always be ready to inflict the same punishment on those who shall disclose this degree and break this obligation. So may God help and maintain me. Amen.

Hiram's assassins get their comeuppance in the 11th degree, when they are ripped open from the chin downward to allow flies to suck their blood. The Royal Arch degree of the York rite is altered and becomes the 13th degree of the Ancient and Accepted Rite. In the final or 14th degree of the Chapter, the candidates agree to assemble at the lodge on December 27, feast of Saint John the Evangelist, and on June 24, feast of Saint John the Baptist.

Masons sometimes point to the 18th degree of the Rose Croix as an example of the "Christian" orientation of the "higher" degrees. We know, however, that Jews, Unitarians, and Muslims are not debarred from any degree in the Scottish rite, and we presume they would not participate in a ceremony that offended their religious beliefs. Incidentally, the candidate is asked, "Do you promise never to consent to the admission into a Chapter of Rose Croix of anyone who is or has been a Monk or Jesuit, or is an Atheist?"

The Rose Croix candidate passes through three apartments, representing Calvary, the scene of the Ascension, and hell. The initiate is warned, "The horrors [of hell] which you have just seen are but a faint representation of those you shall suffer if you break through our laws, or infringe the obligation you have taken."

A Mason who belonged to a Christian church might well be deceived by the symbols used in this ceremony. He sees a cross and may understandably associate this with the Christian religion until he reads in his copy of *Morals and Dogma*:

> The Cross has been a sacred symbol from the earliest Antiquity. It is found upon all the enduring monuments of the world, in Egypt, in Assyria, in Hindostan, in Persia, and on the Buddhist towers of Ireland [!]. Buddha was said to have died upon it. The Druids cut an oak into its shape and held it sacred, and built their temples in that

form. Pointing to the four quarters of the world, it was the symbol of universal nature. It was on a cruciform tree, that Chrishna was said to have expired, pierced with arrows. It was revered in Mexico. But its peculiar meaning in this degree, is that given by the ancient Egyptians.[5]

Well, perhaps the Rose Croix is not the Christian symbol we might have imagined, but what about the Sacred Word of the degree: I.N.R.I.? Again the leading authority on Scottish-rite Masonry enlightens us:

To the word INRI, inscribed on the Crux Ansata over the Master's Seat, many meanings have been assigned. The Christian Initiate reverentially sees in it the initials of the inscription upon the cross on which Christ suffered— *Iesus Nazarenus Rex Iudaeorum.* The sages of Antiquity connected it with one of the greatest secrets of Nature, that of universal regeneration. They interpreted it thus, *Igne natura renovatur integra* (entire nature is renovated by fire). The Alchemical or Hermetic Masons framed for it this aphorism, *Igne nitrum roris invenitur.* And the Jesuits are charged with having applied to it this odious axiom, *Justum necare reges impios.* The four letters are the initials of the Hebrew words that represent the four elements— Iammim, the seas or water; Nour, fire; Rouach, the air, and Iebeschah, the dry earth. How we read it, I need not repeat to you.[6]

On Maundy Thursday, members of the Rose Croix chapters celebrate the Feast of the Paschal Lamb with a one-and-a-half-hour ceremony combining Jewish and Christian elements. Thirteen members wearing dark robes represent participants at the Last Supper and sit at a cross-shaped table.

[5] Pike, *Morals and Dogma*, p. 290.
[6] Ibid., p. 291.

Undoubtedly, the most objectionable degree in the Scottish rite for a Roman Catholic is the 30th, or Grand Elect Knight Kadosh K–H or simple Knight Kadosh in the Southern Jurisdiction. Candidates may skip the previous eleven degrees in order to take the 30th, which is never conferred titularly. Vengeance is the motif of this degree, whose bitterly anti-Catholic tone is absent in the corresponding English workings.

The Thrice Puissant Grand Master charges the candidates: "Your assistance at this juncture is invaluable, as we have crime to punish and innocence to protect. Persecution and oppression are raging. The religious and political rulers of the world will not render that justice which they have sworn to render, and we cannot endure their encroachments any longer." The Grand Master approaches a table that supports three skulls. One skull wears a papal tiara, another a wreath of laurel, and the third a regal crown. The Grand Master stabs the skull with the papal tiara, and the candidate repeats, "Down with Imposture! Down with crime!" Both the Grand Master and candidate kneel before the second skull and chorus, "Everlasting glory to the immortal martyr of virtue." Passing to the third crowned skull, the two repeat, "Down with tyranny! Down with crime!"

The Grand Pontiff addresses the candidate:

You have already been informed that among the Knights Kadosh truth and reality take the place of symbols, and even now your sagacity will partly raise the curtain which cannot be entirely removed until you have sustained new trials. In all the preceding degrees you must have observed that the object of Scotch Masonry is to overthrow all kinds of superstitions, and that by admitting in her bosom on terms of the strictest equality, the members of all religions, of all creeds and of all countries, without any distinction whatever, she has, and indeed can have, but one single object and that is to restore to the Grand Architect of the Universe, to the common father of the human race those who are lost in the maze of impostures, invented for the sole purpose of enslaving them. The Knights Kadosh recognize no particular religion, and for that reason we demand of you nothing more than to worship God. And whatever may be the religious forms imposed upon you by superstition at a period of your life when you were incapable of discerning truth from falsehood, we do not even require you to relinquish them. Time and study alone can enlighten you. But remember that you will never be a true Mason unless you repudiate forever all superstitions and prejudices.

However, until then, you will own that we have required of you nothing more than to acknowledge with us the sole, the only certain and undoubted point admitted as such by all the human race without exception. We mean the existence of a first great cause, whom we call God Almighty.

The candidate now takes his second oath as a Knight Kadosh:

I, ——, solemnly and sincerely promise and swear wholly to devote myself to the emancipation of humanity; to practice toleration, in political and religious matters especially, toward all men. To strive unceasingly for the happiness of my fellow beings, for the propagation of light and for the overthrow of superstition, fanaticism, imposture, and intolerance.

I furthermore solemnly promise and swear to help my brethren even at the peril of my life, if they should be persecuted for their religion, for the holy cause of liberty, or as members of the higher Masonic bodies. So help me God.

The Grand Pontiff now instructs the candidate to toss some incense in the fire burning on the altar of perfumes while he prays, "Almighty Father, Holy and Merciful. Oh! Thou of whom we are the beloved children, accept this incense which we offer thee with our hearts, as a token of love and reverence. May thy kingdom come at last, and with it the end of all fanaticism, intolerance, imposture, and superstition. Amen."

In a subsequent mock balloting on the candidate's fitness, one of the Judges reports, "I have voted in the negative, Sovereign Grand Judge. I have good reason to believe, nay I know, that the candidate entertains anti-Masonic opinions; that is to say, intolerant and sectarian principles, not only in religious but also in Masonic matters." The dissenting Judge asks that the candidate compose a written testament of his profession of faith in Masonry. The candidate complies with this demand, and the document is kept on file in the Scottish-rite Cathedral.

As the Grand Provost of Justice points a sword at the heart of the candidate, he repeats his third oath as Knight Kadosh:

> I, ——, of my own free will and accord, do hereby solemnly and sincerely promise and swear to keep faithfully the secrets of the sublime degree of Knight Kadosh and strictly to obey the statutes of the order.
>
> I further solemnly promise and swear to protect innocence and to punish crime, to help all in distress, to do all in my power to crush oppressors and to defend the oppressed. Every Knight Kadosh shall be to me as if the ties of blood had united us.
>
> I further solemnly promise and swear never to challenge a Knight Kadosh to mortal combat, before having previously submitted my motives to the Council assembled in its Areopagus, and if I were in a place where

no Council existed, to take advice of at least two Knights Kadosh.

I furthermore solemnly promise and swear never to slander a Knight Kadosh, and never to cause him any prejudice either by word or by action. And should I ever infringe or violate any of my obligations I now take, I do from this moment accept and consent to undergo the sentence which may be pronounced against me by this dreaded tribunal, which I hereby acknowledge as my Supreme Judge. All of which I promise to do, under the penalty of death. So help me God.

A large mausoleum in the shape of a pyramid is featured in the fourth apartment, which is hung with red and black draperies. A funeral urn, crowned with laurel and covered by a black veil, rests on a platform of the mausoleum flanked by the papal tiara and the royal crown. Thick incense obscures the interior of the hall, which is illuminated by only five candles. An altar on the west holds a human skull inlaid with silver, a decanter of wine, and a loaf of bread covered by a cloth. A ladder with seven rungs is placed between the mausoleum and the altar.

The candidate for Knight Kadosh is instructed to ascend the ladder. Each step on one side represents a quality such as Justice or Meekness, while the reverse steps stand for a science such as Geometry. Following the fourth oath, the candidate is told, "My brother, you are now convinced that the degree of Knight Kadosh is the apex of the Masonic edifice. It contains all the science of Masonry." Of course, this claim is rejected by the Blue Lodges, which do not even officially acknowledge the existence of degrees other than the basic three.

The Thrice Puissant Grand Master points to the papal tiara and declares:

This represents the tiara of the cruel and cowardly Pontiff, who sacrificed to his ambition the illustrious order of those Knights Templar of whom we are the true successors. A crown of gold and precious stones ill befits the humble head of one who pretends to be the successor, the Vicar, of Jesus of Nazareth. It is therefore the crown of an impostor, and it is in the name of Him who said, "Neither be ye called Masters" that we trample it under our feet.

He asks if the candidate is willing to do this, and then all trample on the pope's crown, brandishing poniards and shouting "Down with Imposture!" Did we understand Pike correctly when he said that men of all races and creeds may take the Scottish-rite degrees without compromising their beliefs? We feel justified in doubting the faith of any Catholic who would insult the emblem of the pope's authority in a lodge ritual.

Earlier in the 30th-degree ritual, the prospective Knights Kadosh are counseled, "And, finally, keep aloof from uniting yourself with any sectional, political, or sectarian religious organization whose principles can in any way bias your mind or judgment, or in the slightest degree trammel with obligations the vows you have just made." This leaves no question of which society, Church or Scottish rite, should claim a man's first loyalty. President Charles A. Blanchard of Wheaton College pointed out, "Not less than five or six times in the dreary monotony of this degree is the candidate given to understand that Christianity is a narrow, fanatical, intolerant system, while Masonry is a broad, comprehensive, generous one, and that if he is a good Mason he must not be a Christian."

This blasphemy is delivered by the Advocate in the working of the 31st degree: "We revolt against the law, by which the crooked limbs and diseased organism of the child are the fruits of the father's vices. We even think that a God, omnipotent and omniscient, ought to have permitted no pain, no poverty, no servitude. Our ideal of justice is more lofty than the actualities of God."

A recital of the lessons of the preceding thirty-one degrees begins the initiation ceremony of the 32nd degree. The candidates are told that "Masonry will eventually rule the world", and they pray for the "universal dominion of the true principles of Masonry".

The chart on page 6 indicates the names of all the degrees in Scottish-rite Masonry. A slightly different arrangement prevails in the Southern jurisdiction. Degrees 15 through 18 are conferred in a Chapter of Rose Croix, 19 through 30 by a Council of Kadosh, and 31 and 32 by a Consistory. In some cases the name of the degree also varies.

The *Encyclopedia Americana* explains, "Though founded on Craft Masonry, the Scottish rite is not so much a branch thereof as it is a separate system of Masonry; entirely so as to organization, and largely so as to doctrine." [7] The Scottish rite is not bound by the Masonic landmark that outlaws discussion of politics and religion in the lodge. As a result, what anti-Catholic propaganda is disseminated in American Freemasonry may usually be traced to the Scottish rite, Southern Jurisdiction. The Mason who has never gone beyond the Blue Lodge may be quite sincere when he testifies that he has never heard a word against the Church in his lodge. But the Southern Jurisdiction Scottish-rite Mason who would make the same statement would be unusually inattentive or else simply evasive.

Other Master Masons may choose to advance through the ten-degree York rite, of which three degrees may be skipped. As the Scottish rite has nothing to do with Scotland, so the York rite has nothing to do with York. A more

[7] *Enyclopedia Americana*, vol. 18, p. 389a.

accurate but less popular term is the American rite, since this combination of degrees is worked only in the United States.

Three preparatory degrees of Mark Master, Past Master (Virtual), and Most Excellent Master culminate in the Royal Arch degree. In England this Royal Arch degree has been considered a complementary degree to the 3rd degree since the 1813 reconciliation. As such it claims to be a part of pure and ancient Masonry. The Royal Arch is the largest body within American Freemasonry. It and the three preceding York-rite degrees are controlled by the General Grand Chapter of Royal Arch Masons of the United States of America.

The quest for the true name of God forms the basis for the Royal Arch degree, which seems to have been introduced into modern Masonry in the 1750s. According to Masonic legend, God's name, revealed to Moses in the burning bush, was known to the Jews until the assassination of Hiram Abiff. At Hiram's death a substitute name, "Mahabone", was invented, but the real name was not discovered until 470 years later in the building of the second temple. JAH-BUL-ON, the supposed lost word, is made up of three ancient names for the deity, the Hebrew Jehovah, the Assyrian Baal, and the Egyptian On, or Osiris. This linking of the sacred name of the God of the Hebrews with the names of two pagan deities shocked even Pike, who wrote, "No man or body of men can make me accept as a sacred word, as a symbol of the infinite and eternal Godhead, a mongrel word, whose name has been for more than two thousand years an appellation of the Devil." He added, "No word has any business in the Royal Arch degree that makes the name of a heathen deity one of the names of the true God."

The lengthy oath, administered by the Principal Sojourner and repeated by the Royal Arch candidate, includes the following statement: "I furthermore promise and swear that I will employ a Companion Royal Arch Mason in preference to any other person of equal qualifications. I furthermore promise and swear that I will assist a Companion Royal Arch Mason when I see him engaged in any difficulty, and will espouse his cause so far as to extricate him from the same, whether he be right or wrong."

Should the York-rite Mason wish, he may apply for the trio of Council degrees: Royal Master, Select Master, and Super Excellent Master, but he can also bypass these and move directly into the Commandery. A class of York-rite candidates may receive the Chapter degrees on a Wednesday evening and Thursday, followed by the Council degrees on Friday night and the Commandery degrees on Saturday.

The top degree of the York rite is the Knights Templar, but the prospective Templar must also enter the Order of the Red Cross and the Order of Knights of Malta. The scene between Christ and Thomas is reenacted in the Knights of Malta ritual; the candidate puts his fingers into the print of nails in the Eminent Commander's hands. The York rite's Red Cross of Constantine corresponds to the honorary 33rd degree of the Scottish rite.

Charting the Course, a booklet published by the Grand Encampment of Knights Templar of the U.S., stresses Templary's commitment to Christianity and makes it obvious why a Jewish Mason would not choose to climb to the top of the York-rite ladder. "Templary is Christian to the core —and we must never allow this fact to escape us for one instant. Our very reason for existence as an organization depends upon our observance of this central fact. Nothing is important in our order that does not relate itself to Christ, the Christian religion and the Christian Church." [8]

---

[8] *Charting the Course*, new and rev. ed. (Chicago: Grand Encampment of Knights Templar of the U.S.A., 1982), p. 7.

Again the official Templar handbook declares: "We must reconsecrate our Cause to Christ and the Christian religion with all the sincerity we possess."[9] And "Templary is founded upon the Christian Religion and the practice of the Christian virtues."[10]

Not a shred of evidence supports the claim that the Masonic Knights Templar represents the modern successor to this suppressed medieval order. A gap of more than five hundred years separates the two orders, but as usual the demands of historical accuracy are not oppressive in Masonic research. The original order was formed to protect Christian pilgrims in the Holy Land. Noblemen entered its ranks and took vows of poverty, chastity, and obedience.

Eventually the income of this quasi-religious order reached huge proportions, and oriental heresies were said to have infected some of the high officials. Grand Knight Jacques de Molay and sixty Knights were arrested in Paris and charged with idolatry. De Molay and fifty-four of the Knights were burned at the stake in 1314; the order was suppressed by Church and State, and its possessions were confiscated. The Masonic imitation was organized in the United States in 1816.

Early in the Templar initiation ceremony, the candidate is seated blindfolded in the Chamber of Reflection. When he removes his hoodwink, he sees a Bible, a bowl of water and napkin, and a skull and crossbones. He is asked to complete a questionnaire that asks, "Should you ever be called upon to draw your sword, will you wield it in the defence of the Christian religion?"

At the conclusion of the Knight Templar's obligation, the new Knight swears, "All this I most solemnly and sincerely

[9] Ibid.
[10] Ibid., p. 6.

promise and vow, with a firm and steadfast resolution to keep and perform the same, binding myself under no less penalty than that of having my head smote off and placed on the highest spire of Christendom, should I ever willfully or knowingly violate any part of this solemn obligation of a Knight Templar, so help me God and keep me steadfast to keep and perform the same."

The candidate drinks wine libations to the memory of "our ancient Grand Master, Solomon, King of Israel", to Hiram, King of Tyre, and to Hiram Abiff. After the third libation, the Eminent Commander reminds the candidates: "Pilgrim, these libations in honor of the illustrious Grand Masters of Ancient Craft Masonry are taken in acknowledgment of our connection with, and veneration for, that ancient and honorable institution; but the order to which you now seek to unite is founded upon the Christian religion and the practice of the Christian virtues; you will therefore attend to a lesson from the holy evangelist." He reads Matthew 26:14–25.

The candidate faces a triangular arrangement of twelve candles to represent the Twelve Apostles. In the center of the table a skull rests on a Bible. In memory of the apostasy of Judas, the candidate is asked to extinguish one of the tapers "and let it teach you this important lesson, that he who would violate his vow or betray his trust is worthy of no better fate than that which Judas suffered."

The fourth libation, to Simon of Cyrene, is drunk from a skull, and the fifth, of pure wine, is drunk to immortality.

> This pure wine I now take in testimony of my belief in the mortality of the body and the immortality of the soul; and as the sins of the whole world were once visited upon the head of our Savior, so may all the sins of the person whose skull this once was, in addition to my own,

be heaped upon my head, and may this libation appear in judgment against me, both here and hereafter, should I ever knowingly or willfully violate this my most solemn vow of a Knight Templar; so help me God and keep me steadfast.

To enforce the fifth libation, the assembled Knights draw swords and point them toward the candidate's throat.

The medieval Knight Templar was received into the order: "In the name of God, and of Mary our dear Lady, and in the name of St. Peter of Rome, and of our father the Pope, and in the name of all the brethren of the Temple, we receive you to all the good works of the order." The Masonic Knights Templar employ the following formula: "By virtue of the high power and authority in me vested as the representative of Hugh de Payens and Geoffrey de St. Omer, I do now dub and create you, ——, a Knight of this most valiant and magnanimous order of Knights Templar."

Some 250,000 Knights Templar are banded together in three hundred Commanderies in the United States, Alaska, Mexico, the Philippine Islands, and the Canal Zone. Knights wear a black military uniform with cocked hat and ostrich feathers, silver and gold belts, and swords. They attend Protestant church services in a body on Ascension Day. Their marching hymn is "Onward, Christian Soldiers".

Some Masons attain the 32nd and 33rd degrees in the Scottish rite and then begin to climb the York-rite ladder, or vice versa. By this time they have invested hundreds of dollars in initiation fees, dues, emblems, assessments, banquets, costumes, travel expenses, and so forth. Most of those who have reached the top degrees in either of the two rites also enter the Shrine.

Our thesis that Freemasonry and Christianity form mutually incompatible systems is neither advanced nor rebutted by the contents of the "higher degrees". Most Masons have no knowledge of these rites, and the Blue Lodges of Craft Masonry simply ignore their existence. Neither the objectionable occultism and paganism of some Scottish-rite degrees nor the Christian coloring of the Knights Templar have anything to do with our argument. To the general public, however, all these assorted rites, allied degrees, and the Shrine are "Masonry", and a basic knowledge of them becomes necessary if we wish to understand the complexities of American Freemasonry.[11]

---

[11] For a discussion of Masonry and civil religion, see "Fraternal Association and Civil Religion: Scottish Rite Freemasonry", by Pamela M. Jolicoeur and Louis L. Knowles, *Review of Religious Research*, fall 1978, pp. 3–22.

CHAPTER V

THE MASONIC RELIGION

Masonry Encompasses All Elements of a Religion of Naturalism

The basic Christian objection to Freemasonry is that the Craft constitutes a religious sect in opposition to the revealed truths of the Gospel.

Clearly whatever constitutes "that Religion in which all men agree", it is not Christianity or revealed religion. Masons as Masons believe in the fatherhood of God, the brotherhood of mankind, and the immortality of the soul. These are beliefs that they maintain can be discovered by human reason. The inspiration of the Bible, the unique claims of Jesus Christ, the authority and teaching role of the Church, and the sacraments as means of grace are "particular opinions" that Freemasons are asked to keep to themselves rather than disturb the brothers in the lodge.

A century ago, in his encyclical on Freemasonry, *Humanum Genus*, Leo XIII defined naturalism, which he saw as the primary objection to the Masonic system: "Now the fundamental doctrine of the Naturalists, which they sufficiently make known by their very name, is that human nature and human reason ought in all things be mistress and guide. . . . For they deny that anything has been taught by God; they allow no dogma of religion or truth which cannot be understood by human intelligence, nor any teacher who ought to be believed by reason of his authority."

In keeping with the naturalism of the lodge, no prayers in the Blue Lodges are ever officially offered in the name of Jesus Christ. God, whom Christians have been told to address as our Father, is worshiped as the deistic Great Architect of the Universe (G.A.O.T.U.).

In Freemasonry, all women, men under the age of twenty-one, and those physically incapable of giving the proper signs of recognition are barred from initiation. Otherwise only the atheist—technically, the "stupid atheist"—and the "irreligious libertine" are unwelcome. By jettisoning the vestiges of Christianity, modern Freemasonry opened its doors to Deists, Jews, Muslims, Hindus, Buddhists, and any who acknowledge the existence of the G.A.O.T.U. and believe in the immortality of the soul. Perhaps a religious naturalism is better than no religious belief at all, but for the professing Christian it represents a retreat from the Gospel.

Not all the religious systems in the world are exclusive; Christianity is. A Chinese may combine elements of Confucianism, Buddhism, and Taoism, and a Japanese may successfully blend Shintoism and Buddhism. A Christian owes complete loyalty to God the Father, Son, and Holy Spirit; he may not divide his allegiance among other gods.

The lodge honors Jesus Christ as it honors Socrates, Buddha, and Muhammed. It cannot acknowledge any special spiritual claims by Jesus, since this would violate the basis of Freemasonry.

Most Masons who deny that Masonry is a religion confuse religion with the Christian religion. They know Masonry is not Christian, since if it were, their Jewish and Muslim brethren would object. Since it is not Christian, they assume that it is not religious. Or their views of Christianity as primarily a system of character building and as synonymous with the decent, kindly, and gentlemanly coincide with their appraisal of the lodge, and they see no conflict between the two institutions. The fact is, however, that the lodge is essentially religious and possesses all the elements of a religion of naturalism.

We can agree with Albert Pike when he wrote: "Every Masonic lodge is a temple of religion and its teachings are instruction in religion."[1] Pike served as Sovereign Grand Inspector of the Southern Jurisdiction of the Scottish rite for many years and is considered American Freemasonry's most eminent philosopher.

Not only does Freemasonry see itself as a religion, but it sees itself as the universal religion, while it considers Christianity as simply another of the dozens of sects whose particular opinions have divided mankind over the ages. Again, we may refer to Pike: "But Masonry teaches, and has preserved in their purity, the cardinal tenets of the old primitive faith, which underlie and are the foundation of all religions. All that ever existed have had a basis of truth; all have overlaid the truth with error."[2] "Religion, to obtain currency and influence with the great mass of mankind, must needs be alloyed with such an amount of error as to place it far below the standard attainable by the higher human capacities."[3]

Masonry, however, strips sectarian religion of these encrusted "errors" and reveals itself as the universal religion. While religion gathers the barnacles of superstition and error, Masonry remains pure and undefiled. It becomes Christianity without Christ, Judaism without the Law, Islam without the Prophet.

---

[1] Albert Pike, *Morals and Dogma* (Charleston, S.C.: Supreme Council of the Thirty-third Degree for the Southern Jurisdiction of the United States, 1881), p. 213.

[2] Ibid., p. 161.

[3] Ibid., p. 224.

In his *Encyclopedia of Freemasonry*, Albert G. Mackey writes:

> I contend, without any sort of hesitation, that Masonry is, in every sense of the word, except one, and that its least philosophical, an eminently religious institution . . . that without this religious element it would scarcely be worthy of cultivation by the wise and good. . . . Who can deny that it is eminently a religious institution? . . . But the religion of Masonry is not sectarian. . . . It is not Judaism, though there is nothing in it to offend a Jew; it is not Christianity, but there is nothing in it repugnant to the faith of a Christian. Its religion is that general one of nature and primitive revelation—handed down to us from some ancient and patriarchal priesthood—in which all men may agree and in which no men can differ. It inculcates the practice of virtue, but supplies no scheme of redemption for sin.[4]

Hannah comments: "On reading the ritual carefully, Masonry will be found to present itself as a complete and self-sufficient system of moral and spiritual guidance through this world and the next. It teaches one's whole duty to God and to man, and a way of justification by works which if followed will lead to salvation. Nowhere does it give the slightest hint that anything further is necessary to the religious life."[5]

While religious, Freemasonry clearly rejects dogma and the possibility of absolute truth. After six years of study, the German Catholic Episcopal Conference reported its conclusions in 1980. On this particular point the German hierarchy observed: "The religious conception of the Mason is

---

[4] Albert G. Mackey, *Encyclopedia of Freemasonry* (Philadelphia: L. H. Everts, 1887), pp. 617–19.

[5] Walton Hannah, *Darkness Visible* (London: Augustine Press, 1952), p. 40.

relativistic: all religions are competitive attempts to explain the truth about God which, in the last analysis, is unattainable. Therefore, only the language of Masonic symbols, which is ambiguous and left to the subjective interpretation of the individual Mason, is adapted to this truth about God."[6]

Some Masonic partisans seem to believe that Masonry could not qualify as a religion because it lacks the complex dogmatic systems of the denominations in their hometown. The lodge demands only belief in a Supreme Architect and in the immortality of the soul. As Mackey states: "The religion of Masonry is pure theism." He boasts, "The truth is that Masonry is undoubtedly a religious institution . . . which, handed down through a long succession of ages from that ancient priesthood who first taught it, embraces the great tenets of the existence of God and the immortality of the soul."[7] In his *Encyclopedia* he restates this: "The Religious Doctrines of Freemasonry are very simple and self-evident. They are darkened by no perplexities of sectarian theology but stand out in broad light, intelligible and acceptable by all minds, for they ask only for a belief in God and in the immortality of the soul."[8]

Mackey explains:

> Although Freemasonry is not a dogmatic theology, and is tolerant in the admission of men of every religious faith, it would be wrong to suppose that it is without a creed. On the contrary, it has a creed, the assent to which it rigidly enforces, and the denial of which is absolutely incompatible with membership in the Order. This creed

---

[6] *Amtsblatt des Erbistums Köln*, June 1980, pp. 102–11.

[7] Albert G. Mackey, *A Text Book of Masonic Jurisprudence* (New York: Maynard, Merrill & Co., 1859), p. 95.

[8] Mackey, *Encyclopedia of Freemasonry*, p. 731.

consists of two articles: First, a belief in God, the Creator of all things, who is therefore recognized as the Grand Architect of the Universe; and secondly, a belief in the eternal life, to which this present life is but a preparatory and probationary state.[9]

Simply because Masonry reduces its theological statement to these two propositions, we may not deduce that it does not constitute a religion. This bare minimum compared to the dogmatic structure of Christianity is nevertheless more than is asked of many religionists: Unitarians, Reform Jews, Buddhists. A Unitarian in good standing may doubt the existence of a personal God and deny the immortality of the soul; his Unitarianism nevertheless constitutes a religion.

Like Unitarianism, the Masonic sect denies the need to accept the Christian Gospel but allows its initiates to entertain their own peculiar theological views outside the lodge room. Human reason becomes the only guide to religious belief, and the Gospel of Christ stands on a par with the scriptures of Hinduism, the Koran, and the Book of Mormon.

The lodge unwittingly confirmed the religious nature of Masonry in a court case in 1903. A certain Robert Kopp, who had been expelled from the fraternity, appealed against his former brethren in the civil courts. He lost his case, but the counsel for the Grand Lodge of New York presented the following statement in his "Briefs and Points":

> The right to membership in the Masonic fraternity is very much like the right to membership in a church. Each requires a candidate for admission to subscribe to certain articles of religious belief as an essential prerequisite to membership. Each requires a member to conduct himself

[9] Ibid., p. 192.

thereafter in accordance with certain religious principles. Each requires its members to adhere to certain doctrines of belief and action. The precepts contained in the "Landmarks and the Charges of a Freemason" formulate a creed so thoroughly religious in character that it may well be compared with the formally expressed doctrine of many a denominational church. The Masonic fraternity may, therefore, be quite properly regarded as a religious society, and the long line of decisions, holding that a religious society shall have sole and exclusive jurisdiction to determine matters of membership, should be deemed applicable to the Masonic fraternity.

Mackey adds:

Look at its ancient landmarks, its sublime ceremonies, its profound symbols and allegories—all inculcating religious observance, and teaching religious truth, and who can deny that it is eminently a religious institution? . . . Masonry, then, is indeed a religious institution; and on this ground mainly, if not alone, should the religious Mason defend it.[10]

Despite the evidence that Masonry displays all the characteristics of a religion, many Masons will deny the obvious and insist that the lodge is religious but not a religion. Contemporary Masonry's most distinguished scholar, Henry Wilson Coil, offers these comments:

Some attempt to avoid the issue by saying that Freemasonry is not a religion but is religious, seeming to believe that the substitution of an adjective for a noun makes a fundamental difference. It would be as sensible to say that man had no intellect but was intellectual or that he had no honor but was honorable. The oft repeated aphorism: "Freemasonry is not a religion, but is most

[10] Ibid., p. 619.

emphatically religion's handmaid," has been challenged as meaningless, which it seems to be.[11]

Coil devotes about fifteen thousand words to the question of Freemasonry and religion. He asks:

Does Freemasonry continually teach and insist upon a creed, tenet, and dogma? Does it have meetings characterized by the practice of rites and ceremonies in and by which its creed, tenet, and dogma are illustrated by myths, symbols, and allegories? If Freemasonry were not a religion, what would have to be done to make it such? Nothing would be necessary or at least nothing but to add more of the same.[12]

The Masonic encyclopedist continues:

That brings us to the real crux of the matter; the difference between a lodge and a church is one of degree and not of kind. Some think that, because it is not a strong or highly formalized or highly dogmatized religion such as the Roman Catholic Church where it is difficult to tell whether the congregation is worshiping God, Christ, or the Virgin Mary, it can be no religion at all. But a church of Friends (Quakers) exhibits even less formality and ritual than a Masonic lodge. The fact that Freemasonry is a mild religion does not mean that it is no religion.[13]

Pike explains:

Masonry, around whose altars the Christian, the Hebrew, the Moslem, the Brahmin, the followers of Confucius and Zoroaster, can assemble as brethren and unite in prayer to the one God who is above all Baalim, must

---

[11] Henry Wilson Coil, *Coil's Masonic Encyclopedia* (New York: Macoy, 1961), p. 512.
[12] Ibid.
[13] Ibid.

needs leave to each of its Initiates to look for the foundation of his faith and hope to the written scriptures of his own religion. For itself it finds those truths definite enough, which are written by the finger of God upon the heart of man and on the pages of the book of nature.[14]

In other words, "for itself" Masonry considers the doctrines of Christianity quite peripheral and quite unnecessary, but if her initiates must look for other sources of religious authority the lodge will not object. At no time, however, does the lodge ever suggest that the religion and morality of the lodge be supplemented by the Church, nor does it direct its initiates to the Church. In fact, those who wish to bypass the Church and find their spiritual sustenance in Masonry alone are welcome to do so and, to be candid about it, are considered much wiser than their brethren who accept the dross and barnacles of Christianity. For many, indeed, the lodge is church enough, and they may testify that they find Freemasonry a completely satisfying spiritual home. Those who desert the Christian Church for the lodge would receive the commendation of the Masonic writer Sir John Cockburn, who said, "Creeds arise, have their day and pass, but Masonry remains. It is built on the rock of truth, not on the shifting sands of superstition." Obviously, those who have chosen the solid truth of the lodge over the superstition and sectarian dogmas of the Church have chosen the better part.

Would the searcher for a religious home find all the elements of a religion in the Masonic lodge? Unquestionably, he would.

He would worship the Great Architect of the Universe in a temple whose lodge room features two chief articles of

[14] Pike, *Morals and Dogma*, p. 226.

worship, an altar and a Volume of the Sacred Law, usually but not necessarily the Bible. Surely, if Masonry were nothing but a mutual benefit society, it would have no need for an altar. True, other fraternal and service organizations appoint chaplains and include prayers in their meetings, but the claims to a superior path to spiritual advancement and a superior morality are peculiar to Freemasonry.

Mackey tells us:

> From all this we see that the altar in Masonry is not merely a convenient article of furniture, intended, like a table, to hold a Bible. It is a sacred utensil of religion, intended, like the altars of the ancient temples, for religious uses, and thus identifying Masonry, by its necessary existence in our Lodges, as a religious institution. Its presence should also lead the contemplative Mason to view the ceremonies in which it is employed with solemn reverence, as being part of a really religious worship.[15]

Every U.S. lodge works with an open Bible on its altar, and to some Masons this seems to affirm its Christian orientation. The preferred term and the one used in English Freemasonry is the Volume of the Sacred Law (V.S.L.). That no special authority is attached to the Old and New Testaments is clear, since a lodge of Muslims may substitute the Koran, a predominantly Hindu lodge the Vedas, and so on. As the *Digest of Masonic Law* makes clear:

> To say that a candidate profess a belief in the divine authority of the Bible is a serious innovation in the very body of Masonry. The Jews, the Chinese, the Turks, each reject either the Old or the New Testament, or both, and yet we see no good reason why they should not be made Masons. In fact, Blue Lodge Masonry has nothing whatever to do

[15] Mackey, *Encyclopedia of Freemasonry*, p. 60.

with the Bible; it is not founded on the Bible. If it was, it would not be Masonry; it would be something else.[16]

Again we turn to Pike:

The Bible is an indispensable part of the furniture of a Christian lodge only because it is the sacred book of the Christian religion. The Hebrew Pentateuch in a Hebrew Lodge, and the Koran in a Mohammedan one, belong on the Altar; and one of these, and the Square and Compass, properly understood, are the Great Lights by which a Mason must walk and work. The obligation of the candidate is always to be taken on the sacred book or books of his religion, that he may deem it more solemn and binding; and therefore it was that you are asked of what religion you were. We have no other concern with your religious creed.[17]

The Bible in the lodge room is not a standard of religious belief but a symbol of a religious attitude toward life. The central allegory of Freemasonry, the assassination of Hiram Abiff, is nowhere recorded in the Bible. The lodge usually picks for its liturgy passages from the Bible that do not mention Christ, lest his name scandalize non-Christian Masons.

Our religious inquirer would know that each candidate for the lodge, in Anglo-Saxon jurisdictions, must affirm belief in a Supreme Architect and in immortality. The shock of entrance of the first degree serves as his Masonic baptism or rebirth as he moves from self-acknowledged darkness and helplessness into the light of Masonic teaching. Mackey describes the shock of entrance in the following words:

There he stands without our portals, on the threshold of this new Masonic life, in darkness, helplessness, and igno-

---

[16] George Wingate Chase, *Digest of Masonic Law*, p. 207.
[17] Pike, *Morals and Dogma*, p. 11.

rance. Having been wandering amid the errors and covered over with the pollutions of the outer and profane
world, he comes inquiringly to our doors, seeking the
new birth, and asking a withdrawal of the veil which
conceals divine truth from his uninitiated sight. . . .
There is to be, not simply a change for the future, but
also an extinction of the past; for initiation is, as it were, a
death to the world and a resurrection to a new life. . . .
The world is left behind—the chains of error and ignorance which have previously restrained the candidate in
moral and intellectual captivity are broken—the portals
of the Temple have been thrown widely open, and Masonry stands before the neophyte in all the glory of its
form and beauty, to be fully revealed to him, however,
only when the new birth has been completely accom-
plished.[18]

Masonry makes no references to that baptism which
makes the Christian a participant in God's own life, to the
sacraments of the Church, to the revealed truths of the Gospel. All men alike come to the portals of the Masonic temple
as aimless wanderers ignorant of divine truths.

We can only speculate on what goes through the mind of
a born-again Christian who approaches the entrance to the
lodge and must confess that he "has long been in darkness,
and now seeks to be brought to light". He may have accepted Jesus Christ as his Lord and Savior, but to the brothers of the lodge he remains in "darkness". As a matter of fact,
Masonry's easy dismissal of the candidate's religious experience prior to his request to join the lodge has stiffened the
opposition of evangelical Protestants. Since such conservative and fundamentalist Protestants now comprise as much as
25 percent of the churchgoing population, Freemasonry has

---

[18] Albert G. Mackey, *Masonic Ritualist* (New York: Clark & Maynard,
1869), p. 23.

seen its recruiting base in U.S. Protestantism drastically contract in recent years.

During the degree workings, the initiate has bound himself by solemn oaths taken on the V.S.L. and asked God himself to witness his resolve to keep the secrets of the order and to enter into specific relationship with his new brethren. All the ritual, prayers, hymns, candles, and vestments of a liturgical church are his in the temple.

The Craft also furnishes him with a moral code that makes no reference to other religions or to models of conduct except those of the Masonic hero: Hiram Abiff. At no time is the Christian Mason encouraged to pattern his life after his Savior or to cultivate the specifically Christian virtues.

His Masonic mentors assure him that fidelity to the principles of the lodge will win him entry to "Thy lodge on high". In explaining the term "Acacian", Mackey explains that this refers to "a Mason who by living in strict accord with his obligations is free from sin".[19] The Mason wins salvation, not through the passion and death of Jesus Christ, but through the mythical assassination and resurrection of Hiram Abiff. He knows that when he dies he will be clothed in the Masonic apron and buried by his brethren. They will assure his survivors that if he has lived according to Masonic principles he will enjoy the bliss of heaven. After the religious services, if any, the lodge takes charge of the graveside ceremony.

All of the pallbearers must be Masons, who typically wear their lambskin aprons, white gloves, and high hats. Neither the church nor any other organization may participate in the Masonic service. Coil observes:

> A man may be born without religious ceremony; he may be married without religious ceremony; but one moment

[19] Ibid., p. 16.

comes to every man when he feels the need of that missing thing—when he comes to crossing into the great beyond. Freemasonry has a religious service to commit the body of a deceased brother to the dust whence it came and to speed the liberated spirit back to the Great Source of Light. Many Freemasons make this flight with no other guarantee of a safe landing than their belief in the religion of Freemasonry. If that is a false hope, the Fraternity should abandon funeral services and devote its attention to activities where it is sure of its ground and its authority.[20]

Masonry meets all the essential requirements of a religion. It is not Christianity, but it is religion. Mackey states:

> Speculative Masonry, now known as Freemasonry, is, therefore, the scientific application and the religious consecration of the rules and principles, the technical language and the implements and materials, of operative Masonry to the worship of God as the Grand Architect of the Universe, and to the purification of the heart and the inculcation of the dogmas of a religious philosophy.[21]

Man arrives at an understanding of this religious philosophy through reason alone, says Masonry. Consequently, this religion of naturalism never rises above the level of any of the non-Christian "higher" religions. For some, a blending of Masonry and their own religion may be a possibility; most Christians do not believe such spiritual bigamy is an option.

Whether to worship the G.A.O.T.U. or the triune God does not pose a dilemma for the Roman Catholic, since he knows that his Church has delineated the incompatibility of the Church and the lodge for more than 250 years. Tens of

---

[20] Coil, *Encyclopedia*, p. 512.
[21] Mackey, *Masonic Ritualist*, p. 75.

millions of Eastern Orthodox and Protestants also belong to churches that forbid any compromise with the lodge.

The problem of dual membership in lodge and church weighs heaviest on those evangelical Protestants, particularly ministers, who attempt to combine the religious tenets of Christianity with those of Masonic naturalism, who try to serve Hiram Abiff and Jesus Christ on alternate evenings. As the Lutheran writer Pastor Theodore Graebner put it, "The difficulty for a Christian remaining a Freemason, then, consists in this, that Christ is not satisfied to share His homage with Allah and with Buddha." [22]

In practically every respect, Masonry resembles the mystery religions and as such represents, not Christianity, but a return to paganism. Mackey states that Masonry "is not Christianity, but there is nothing repugnant to the faith of a Christian".[23] But this is the point: Masonry is admittedly and obviously religious, but it is not Christianity, and this in itself is repugnant to the faith of a Christian.

---

[22] Theodore Graebner, *Is Masonry a Religion?* (St. Louis: Concordia, 1946), p. 60.

[23] Mackey, *Encyclopedia of Freemasonry*, p. 641.

CHAPTER VI

THE MASONIC OATHS

Do They Meet Requirements for a Valid Extrajudicial Oath?

Christians have always regarded an oath, the calling upon God to witness the truth of a statement, as a most serious act of religion. In fact, some Christians, such as the Quakers and the Mennonites, following a literal interpretation of Christ's injunction "Do not swear at all" (Mt 5:33–37), refuse to swear any oath, even in a court of law. Catholics and the majority of other Christians do not interpret this scriptural passage as an absolute prohibition against oaths but as an ideal to be realized in a Christian society where oaths would be unnecessary. Nevertheless, moral theologians emphasize the gravity of an oath and insist that certain conditions be met before a Christian may swear an oath without being guilty of taking the name of the Lord in vain.

Because of the failure to meet these conditions in the Masonic lodge, the Church objects to the solemn obligations or oaths exacted from the candidate for the Blue Lodge degrees. We have described the Blue Lodge initiations in chapter 3 and have given the three oaths of Entered Apprentice (pp. 49–50), Fellow Craft (pp. 57–58), and Master Mason (pp. 62–65). We will not repeat these oaths but invite the reader to refresh his memory by reviewing them as presented in context. Nor will we examine the many oaths in the Scottish and York rites, since these rites do not form an integral part of pure and ancient Masonry.

The Christian objection to the Shriner's obligation taken "upon this Bible" and on the mysterious legend of the Koran and its dedication to the Islamic faith (pp. 129–30) is obvious to all but the most insensitive. The Shriner gives his oath "upon this sacred book, by the sincerity of the Moslem's oath", and concludes by beseeching, "Allah, the god of Arab Moslem and Mohammedan, the god of our fathers, support me to the entire fulfillment of the same. Amen. Amen. Amen." A few Protestant Masons have attempted to defend the Blue Lodge oaths as permissible, but, to my knowledge, no one has risked his theological reputation by trying to justify the oath of the Mystic Shrine.

The chief objection of the Church to the Masonic oath is that it fails to meet the essential requirement for a valid extrajudicial oath, namely, that the matter of the oath be of a serious nature. To call upon the Almighty to witness an oath concerning some trifle is to take the name of God in vain. Actually, what the Masonic candidates swear to conceal is nothing more than a few passwords, secret grips, and lodge rites.

Masonry may be entitled to preserve harmless secrets in order to heighten the interest of prospective members and amuse the brethren. It may employ passwords to exclude the merely curious from its assemblies. But to suggest that the oaths demanded of the candidate are needed to protect such secrets is ridiculous. A gentleman's promise would serve as well, and this is all that other "secret societies", such as the Knights of Columbus, expect.

A family may keep certain secrets within the family circle, but can we imagine the father gathering his children around the family altar, blindfolding them, and asking them to place their hands on the Holy Bible and to declare that they would have their toes split one by one, their hair pulled out by the roots, and their legs tied in a bow knot rather than reveal that the front-door key is usually kept under the doormat?

We can have no doubt that the Masonic oaths are meant to be solemn and binding in a religious sense. The candidate takes them in a lodge opened in the name of God and the Holy Saints John. He takes them kneeling before the altar of Masonry with his hands on the Volume of the Sacred Law, usually a Bible. In fact, he does everything but sign his name with his own blood. Not even in a courtroom, where he is asked to take an oath as a witness, is he asked to demonstrate his sincerity to a greater degree than in the lodge room.

We can see that the Entered Apprentice oath pertains mainly to secrecy, while the second and third involve obligations toward the brethren in the lodge. The candidate freely consents to the most horrible mutilations and punishments should he ever reveal any of the secrets of the lodge. By the time he has become a full-fledged Master Mason, he has agreed to have his throat cut, his tongue torn out by the roots, his body buried in the sands of the sea, his breast torn open, his heart plucked out and devoured by vultures, his body sliced in two, his bowels removed and burned to ashes, and the ashes scattered to the four winds should he ever violate so much as one iota of his obligation. He emphasizes, "All this I solemnly swear . . . without any hesitation, mental reservation, or secret evasion of mind whatever."

Hannah poses the basic dilemma of the Masonic oaths when he writes, "Either the oaths mean what they say, or they do not. If they do mean what they say, then the candidate is entering into a pact consenting to his own murder by barbarous torture and mutilation should he break it. If they do not mean what they say, then he is swearing high-sounding schoolboy nonsense on the Bible, which verges on blasphemy." [1]

Of course, the standard Masonic rejoinder is that although the pledge to secrecy is to be observed absolutely, the punishments themselves are to be understood in a symbolic sense. And yet the candidate has declared that he is swearing the oaths "without hesitation, mental reservation, or secret evasion of mind", and it would seem to most people that to understand these mutilations and murder as symbolic is not the plain meaning of the text. Further, even the symbolic sense is quite contrary to the laws of the land, which do not tolerate murder or mutilation for disclosing a password. If these are the symbolic punishments for disclosing a password, what are the symbolic punishments for treason and grand larceny and rape?

"But you are taking this whole business of the oath too seriously", sigh the Masonic defenders. And this is the whole point: a Christian cannot study the New Testament and come to any conclusion but that only a serious reason will force him to swear an oath. Not only are the secrets of Masonry trivial by nature, but they are common knowledge among those who take the time and trouble to investigate them.

This brings up the interesting point that almost every past and present lodge officer has violated his Entered Apprentice oath, wherein he pledges that he would not "print, paint, stamp, stain, cut, carve, mark, or engrave them [the arts, parts, or points of Ancient Free Masonry], or cause the same to be done, on anything movable or immovable, capable of receiving the least impression of a word, syllable, letter, character, whereby the same may become legible or intelligible to any person under the canopy of heaven, and the

---

[1] Walton Hannah, *Darkness Visible* (London: Augustine Press, 1952), p. 21.

secrets of Masonry thereby unlawfully obtained through my unworthiness." But in order to conduct the lengthy Masonic initiations and to memorize their respective parts, the officers are obliged to purchase and study copies of *Ecce Orienti* or *King Solomon's Temple*, or such rituals as Duncan's and Ronayne's, which are furnished by Masonic supply houses.[2] In so doing, they would at least be accessories to the crime.

The triviality of the matter of the Masonic oath is not the sole objection that the Church raises. She also declares the oath immoral in that it binds the candidate in uncertain things. Like King Herod, the candidate gives his solemn word in things that are hidden to him. Herod discovered that Salome wanted the head of Saint John the Baptist, and the Masonic candidate may find out that he has entered a mystery cult that denies any place to his Savior, that practices a death-and-resurrection rite in the 3rd degree, and that makes demands he is not able to meet.

The Bible speaks of just such oaths and points out that it does not matter whether the thing involved is good or evil: "If anyone utters with his lips a rash oath to do evil or to do good, any sort of rash oath that men swear, and it is hidden from him, when he comes to know it, he shall in any of these be guilty. When a man is guilty in any of these, he shall confess the sin he has committed" (Lev 5:4–5).

Finally, we must state that from the standpoint of moral theology, Masonry has no right to impose an oath on its initiates. That right is reserved to the Church and to legitimate civil authorities. The lodge has no more right to administer such an oath than the Mau Mau or the Chinese tongs. Nor has the lodge any right to keep secrets from legitimate authority in the political or spiritual areas.

---

[2] See the bibliography at the end of this book.

The Masonic oaths are taken under false pretenses and are therefore null and void. The Master assures the candidate that nothing in the oath will interfere with "the duty you owe to your God, your neighbor, your country, or self". But the Christian knows that "no one comes to the Father, but by me" and that in worship he must honor the Son of God, Jesus Christ, who is ignored by lodge religion. He may indeed belong to a Christian denomination that forbids lodge affiliation, and by accepting initiation he is severing his church affiliation. Of what value then are the Master's assurances? When the candidate realizes that his oath has interfered with his duties toward God, he need not consider the oath as binding in conscience.

How inconsistent would be the Church to devote homilies to the evils of taking the name of the Lord in vain and to recite the divine praises in reparation for sins of blasphemy, while at the same time allowing her sons to participate in solemn religious rites centering on oaths to conceal the passwords "Boaz" and "Shibboleth" and "Tubal Cain" and a few knuckle jabs and lodge ceremonies!

At least the Grand Orients do not fall under the condemnation of the Church because of their oaths. They reject a belief in God and simply ask the candidate to promise on the Constitutions of the lodge.

Christians of all denominations know that "You shall not take the name of the Lord your God in vain" (Dt 5:11). They will consent to swear an oath in court and under certain other circumstances, but they know that a sacred oath is not a suitable stage prop for a lodge initiation. Because the Masonic oath violates the conditions for a valid extrajudicial oath, the Church must condemn the oath and the sect that imposes it.

CHAPTER VII

ALLIED MASONIC ORGANIZATIONS

Shrine, DeMolay, Eastern Star Limited to Masons and Relatives

The 610,000 red-fezzed Shriners revel in Islamic shenanigans, sponsor boisterous national conventions, and raise millions of dollars to support their twenty-two hospitals for crippled and burned children. In size and prestige, the Shrine tops the list of some sixty allied Masonic organizations in this country.

This extensive network of Masonic-related associations includes some for Masons, their wives, sons, daughters, and relatives; for Masons in college and in the armed forces; and for Masons interested in the history of the Craft, social activities, ancient rites, charities, writing, and Masonic philosophy. None of these threescore groups constitutes an official Masonic society, since pure Masonry is confined to the three Symbolic or Blue-Lodge degrees. But they are all limited in membership to Masons and their relatives, and all promote the interests of the lodge.

Membership in the Ancient Arabic Order Nobles of the Mystic Shrine is open only to men who are Knights Templar or 32nd-degree Masons in the Scottish rite.

A group of thirteen Masons in New York had been meeting weekly for luncheon in the early 1870s. They chafed under the solemn decorum of the lodge and sought more fun and frolic than American Freemasonry would tolerate. From this informal luncheon group emerged the Ancient Arabic Order Nobles of the Mystic Shrine. Two men, a physician and a stage comedian, co-founded the Shrine, and one of these, to the chagrin of later generations of Shriners, died a Catholic and was buried from a Catholic church.

The physician, Dr. Walter M. Fleming, composed most of the Shrine ritual, which Father Walton Hannah, an expert in Masonic history and rituals, has called an "adolescent and occasionally Rabelaisian nadir of driveling tomfoolery and burlesque blasphemies". Dr. Hubert M. Poteat, a past imperial potentate, has observed: "Little boys play cops and robbers; Shriners play Moslems and infidels."

Dr. Fleming invented most of the outlandish titles of the Mystic Shrine and its "fun" features that have made it the "playground of Masonry". He also insisted that the new organization admit only 32nd-degree Masons or Knights Templar. At this time, however, he was only a Master Mason himself, so the Shrine organization was not completed until the doctor could also win his 32nd degree. By setting up the Masonic requirement, the founders sought simply to limit membership to men of some financial and social stature; in no sense did they imagine they were inventing a superior Masonic degree or rite.

Mecca Temple in New York City was organized as the first Shrine temple (1872) and therefore can be called the Mother Church of a new fraternity for Masons in which fun and fellowship would be stressed more than ritual.

In later years Dr. Fleming elaborated the legend that the Shrine was really the modern extension of an Arabic vigilante group that had been founded by Kalif Alee, son-in-law of the Prophet Muhammed, in A.D. 656. He added bits and pieces to the legend for years and developed into such a liar that he could no longer distinguish between fact and myth. His "history" of the Shrine is totally unreliable.

Fleming carried on a lucrative medical practice for many years, but he dabbled in every imaginable Masonic enterprise; his wife divorced him, and he died penniless. His grandson would one day write: "My mother opposed my entering the Masons. I think she felt that my grandfather had dissipated a fortune in the various orders he served." After 1886 Fleming dropped out of active participation in the Shrine. He died in 1913.

His friend and co-founder was the Bob Hope of his day: Billy Florence. He was born William J. Conlin in 1831, the son of Irish immigrants. He turned to the stage, took the name "Billy Florence", and attained great popularity as a comedian. Perhaps unaware of the Church's injunctions against the Masonic lodge, Billy Florence joined a Masonic lodge in Philadelphia in 1853. A rather lukewarm Mason, he was twice suspended for nonpayment of dues, from 1857 to 1863 and again from 1868 to 1871.

When Billy Florence fell ill in Philadelphia—long after he had helped found the Shrine—his relatives summoned a priest to his bedside; his wife, a Catholic, was visiting in England at the time. Father Flanagan of Saint Mary's Church heard his confession and gave absolution. Since it was well known that Florence was a Mason, he must have renounced the lodge. Billy Florence was buried from Saint Agnes Church at 43rd off Lexington in New York, to which church he had once contributed $15,000. The pastor told a reporter for the *New York Sun*: "Mr. Florence was a good Catholic at heart. . . . Billy Florence was a noble man, and I am sure that when he became a Mason he did not do so with the idea of being contrary to his church."

The Grand Lodge of New York announced that Florence

would receive no Masonic honors at his funeral, since he had received the last rites of the Church. Nevertheless, the Shrine did send a floral piece featuring the square-and-compass emblem. The Shriners could not believe that Billy Florence had left the lodge, and Dr. Fleming, who had not been present at the end, assured his Masonic brothers that Florence had been duped or drugged. (Some parallels could be drawn between the lives of Billy Florence and a later song-and-dance man, George M. Cohan. Like Florence, Cohan was baptized a Catholic and joined the Masonic lodge, Scottish rite, and Shrine but returned to the Church before his death.)

Following in the footsteps of Billy Florence, a number of show-business personalities have become Shriners, including Red Skelton, Gene Autry, and Ernest Borgnine.

The early growth of the Shrine was slow. By 1878, membership had reached 425 in thirteen temples. These early Shriners won an unenviable reputation as tipplers; they referred to booze as "camel's milk". Some state Masonic Grand Lodges debated whether to expel any Masons who joined the Shrine.

For its first fifty years, the Mystic Shrine went its jolly way, supplementing the austerity of the lodge room with the conviviality, horseplay, and refreshments of the Ancient Arabic Order. By the time of the 1920 Shrine convention, some of the Nobles were voicing their concern over the poor image of the organization and its lack of serious purpose. It was then proposed that the Shrine build a hospital for the care of crippled children. This hospital was to be open only to those who were unable to pay; it would be financed through a two-dollar-a-year assessment on all Shriners. The Shriners' hospital would admit those of all creeds and races. This was a basic departure from the Masonic principle of Masonic charity for Masons and their families; some of the members objected to the plan on this basis.[1]

Envy of the Catholic Church's role in building and staffing hundreds of hospitals across the country was an obvious factor in the debate on the proposal at the 1920 convention. Forrest Adair of Atlanta declared:

> I hope that within two, or three, or four or five years from now we will be impelled from the wonderful work that has been done, to establish more of these hospitals, in easy reach of all parts of North America, and let it be known that while our friends, the enemy, is now about the only institution that is establishing hospitals and schools and things of that kind for the benefit of humanity, the Shrine is going to do them one better.

No one in Noble Adair's audience had any doubt as to the identity of "the enemy". To allay the fears of the Nobles, another speaker assured them that if the hospital committee did not "do it right and devoted themselves too much to Catholic children or Negro children we can fire them and get another committee."

The hospital proposal passed, and the first patient was admitted in 1922. This was the beginning of one of the most admirable philanthropic enterprises in the country: the twenty-two Shrine hospitals for crippled children and burn victims. Admission is based solely on medical and financial need. Free medical treatment is given from infancy to the age of eighteen, regardless of race, religion, or relationship to a Shriner. Nineteen of these institutions are orthopedic units, and the other three treat burns.

[1] For the early history of the Shrine hospitals, see Fred Van Deventer, *Parade to Glory: The Story of the Shriners and Their Hospitals for Crippled Children* (New York: William Morrow, 1959).

Each Shriner pays an assessment to care for the approximately thirteen thousand children admitted each year. Since 1922, more than three hundred fifty thousand crippled and burned children have been treated without charge. The Shriners also raise funds from the general public through their sponsorship of circuses, the East-West Shrine game, sporting events, horse shows, and the like.

The Shrine took a public-relations body blow in 1986 when the *Orlando* (Florida) *Sentinel* revealed that less than one-third of the millions raised each year through such fund-raising activities as the circuses was actually given to the hospitals. The rest was spent on travel, food, ceremonials, and entertainment for the Shriners themselves.[2] *Newsweek* magazine commented: "Charity, wrote Oscar Wilde, creates a multitude of sins. For the Shriners, it also seems to have inspired high living." The magazine added: "The report [in the *Orlando Sentinel*] was so well documented that Shrine officials could not ignore its conclusions. Instead, they promised to reprimand members who misrepresented fund-raising efforts."[3]

Not only have thousands of youngsters benefited from the free medical treatment at these Shriners' hospitals, but the adoption of the hospital program has tapped the idealism of the members and won far more sympathy from the public than an organization devoted only to high jinks and drinking could ever hope to achieve.

President Warren G. Harding became the first president to wear the Shriner's fez. Later, Presidents Roosevelt, Truman, and Ford would also join the Shrine. Four heads of the Mexican government—Porfirio Díaz, Pascual Ortiz Rubio, Abelardo L. Rodríguez, and Miguel Alemán Valdés—have been

[2] Associated Press report, June 30, 1986.
[3] *Newsweek*, July 14, 1986, p. 41.

members of the Mystic Shrine, as was King Kalakaua of Hawaii.[4]

By some serious Freemasons, the Shrine is often dismissed as an incredibly vulgar and frivolous organization that has sapped the strength of the American lodges. They complain that men enter the Blue Lodges and the rites only in order to meet the requirements of the Shrine. The Grand Lodge of England, mother lodge of world Freemasonry, disdains the Shrine and threatens to expel any English Freemason who joins its ranks.

Chief officer of a local temple is the Illustrious Grand Potentate. He wears a purple velvet robe whose sleeves are trimmed with gold braid, a gold sash, a purple-and-yellow turban, and a jeweled scepter with a crescent at the top. His Jewel of Office, worn on the left breast, is a pyramid with a gold sun and rays and a frowning face. The other officials bear similar grandiloquent titles: the Illustrious Chief Rabban, the Illustrious Most High Prophet and Priest, the Illustrious Oriental Guide, and so on.

The interior of the Shrine temple is usually draped in black or in white edged with purple and blue. The furniture includes an Altar of Obligation on which there is a Koran and a Bible, the Black or Holy Stone, which is about one foot square, and two crossed swords. Incense burns on the Altar of Incense. There are also a canopy or tent in a cart and a pedestal with a gavel and a large scimitar.

As many as three hundred candidates "cross the burning sands" at one time in the initiations held at least once a year in the Shrine temples in the U.S., Canada, Mexico, and Panama. Candidates for initiation take off their coats and shoes and put on white dominoes and slippers. They are

---

[4] *Ancient Arabic Order Nobles of the Mystic Shrine: A Short History* (Tampa, Fla.: Shrine General Office, n.d.).

handcuffed or tied loosely at the wrist. After a certain amount of ceremony, the Oriental Guide declares:

> Illustrious Grand Potentate, 'tis I who have ushered in these poor Sons of the Desert, who being weary of the hot sands and burning sun of the plains, humbly crave that sacred boon to the weary and thirsty traveler, a cup of water and shelter under the protecting dome of our goodly temple. I do commend them to your favor, having found them worthy and not of treacherous or ignoble purpose, each having passed the ordeal to the secret ballot of our Mystic Shrine unsoiled and vouched for by a Noble with our secret pass.

They are marched around the lodge room to the station of the Illustrious Most High Prophet and Priest. He asks several questions, including "Have you a belief in the existence of a Deity, future rewards and punishments?" "Have you a desire to promote justice and suppress wrong?" "Have you due regard for female virtue?" And "Are you willing to jeopardize your life, if need be, to punish the guilty and protect the innocent and labor in the cause of justice, truth, and common humanity?"

The High Priest emphasizes the supposed antiquity of the Mystic Shrine and the requirement of absolute secrecy. He ends his discourse by welcoming the Sons of the Desert: "By the existence of Allah and the creed of Mohammed; by the legendary sanctity of our Tabernacle at Mecca, we greet you, and in commemoration of the Arab's faith in purity and innocence, we accept your answers as sincere, and you will now be permitted to proceed in the rites and ceremonies of the Mystic Shrine."

The Chief Rabban, Grand Potentate, and Priest recite short verses before the candidates are asked to kneel at the Altar of Obligation and repeat the following oath:

I, ——, of my voluntary desire, uninfluenced and of free accord do hereby assume, without reserve, the Obligations of the Nobility of the Mystic Shrine, as did the elect of the Temple of Mecca, the Moslem and the Mohammedan. I do hereby, upon this Bible, and on the mysterious legend of the Koran, and its dedication to the Mohammedan faith, promise and swear and vow on the faith and honor of an upright man, come weal or woe, adversity or success, that I will never reveal any secret part or portion whatsoever of the ceremonies I have already received, that are about to be communicated to me and that I may hereafter be instructed in, to any person in the world, except it be known to be a well-known member of the Order of Nobles of the Mystic Shrine, and I, knowing to an absolute certainty that he or they may be truly and lawfully such, and of good standing with such Nobility. That I will not be present, aid or countenance the conferring of the Order of the Mystic Shrine upon any person who is not a Masonic Knight Templar or a thirty-second degree A. and A. Scottish Rite Mason in good standing.

I further promise and vow that I will not willfully write, cut, speak or portray any detail that might be construed into even a clue to the same, except for official Temple work.

Furthermore, I do here register a sacred vow, promising, should I live to become a member, I will impartially cast a black ballot without fear of favor against friend or foe applying for membership in the Nobility of the Mystic Shrine, whom I believe to be disgraced, dishonored, a thief, a perjurer, a murderer, a lunatic, an idiot or a criminal. [*Author's note: the candidate has just declared a few seconds ago that only Masons may join the Shrine!*] And should I undismayed pass safely through the Moslem test and be found worthy of the confidence of my fellows albeit I do not actively espouse the cause, still I do promise to be silent, even if neutral, and not oppose the purposes of the order.

I further promise and vow that I will obey the laws and submit to the decrees of the Parent Temple, the Imperial Grand Council of the United States of America, and that I will not acknowledge, recognize nor be present in any other body of Nobles of the Mystic Shrine, claiming to be superior in authority, nor be present in any clandestine Temple not holding constitutional authority from the Imperial Grand Council of the Mystic Shrine.

I furthermore promise and vow that to the full measure of my ability I will never swerve from justice nor duty. That I will respect virtue; protect the innocent; assist the distressed; promise the inculcation of honor and integrity and dispense reasonable charity. That I will protect and defend the unsullied honor of any Noble of the Mystic Shrine, when absent, if assailed; and now upon this sacred book, by the sincerity of a Moslem's oath I here register this irrevocable vow, subscribing myself bound thereto as well as binding myself by the obligation of the prerequisite to this membership, that of a Knight Templar or that of a 32nd-degree A. and A. Scottish Rite Mason. In willful violation whereof may I incur the fearful penalty of having my eyeballs pierced to the center with a three-edged blade, my feet flayed and I be forced to walk the hot sands upon the sterile shores of the Red Sea until the flaming sun shall strike me with livid plague, and may Allah, the god of Arab Moslem and Mohammedan, the god of our fathers, support me to the entire fulfillment of the same. Amen. Amen. Amen.

At the conclusion of this oath, the prospective Nobles are asked to kiss the Christian Bible. The Priest then declares: "Unbind the Sons of the Desert. They are now of noble birth. The rays of the hot, flaming sun upon the sterile shores of the Red Sea are strong and more scathing than the hempen thong."

The candidates now face "the Moslem test of courage". In large classes, only a few are chosen to undergo this hazing. These pranks are similar to those practiced by college fraternities in their initiations.

Among the pranks engineered during the remainder of the initiation is the "bunghole test", in which two blindfolded candidates enter opposite ends of a large metal cylinder and bump heads in the middle. As the two participants lie down for a minute's rest after this ordeal, one of the Nobles yelps like a small dog while another squirts a few drops of warm water in the candidate's face. A fellow Noble indignantly demands, "Take that dog out of here. He has just p—— in the face of Mr. ——!" Other candidates are instructed to stoop low to receive the Grand Salaam, which consists of a blow by two pieces of board that are set to explode small torpedoes on contact.

Now another candidate for the Nobility is stripped to shirt, drawers, and slippers and led around the room several times. Finally the Conductor says, "This is the place where our brethren stop to sprinkle the Devil's Pass with urine. You will contribute a few drops of urine to commemorate the time and place where all who pass here renounce the wiles and evils of the world to worship at the Shrine of Islam. Only a few drops will do." As the candidate begins to comply, his blindfold is jerked off, and he beholds a group of women (disguised Nobles) staring at him. He retreats in confusion. Later the Nobles stage a mock hanging and beheading and pretend to drink the blood from the severed head. The initiation closes with a banquet.

Shrine membership peaked in 1979 at 942,000, and the organization has lost about 330,000 Nobles since then. The average age of a Shriner is sixty-two, and the annual drop in membership has averaged 28,000 since 1990. Initiation fees, dues, and assessments are relatively expensive, and most Masons never go on to the York or Scottish rites, a prerequisite for initiation. To maintain Shrine membership, a Noble must pay dues not only to the Shrine but to the Blue Lodge and to the York or Scottish rites. Some Shrine officials have recently suggested dropping the Masonic requirement, but such a change is unlikely in the near future.

A number of the 178 Shrine temples still report substantial memberships. The largest, Murat Temple in Indianapolis, had 23,000 members in 1985 and is down to 15,000; between 600 and 800 die or drop out each year. The various temples sponsor glee clubs, bands, and drill teams; some own camels and operate country clubs and athletic facilities. Wives and female relatives of Shriners have organized the Daughters of the Nile (81,000) and the smaller Ladies Oriental Shrine of North America (32,000).

Master Masons make whoopee in the fun organizations of the Blue Lodges: the Grotto and the Forests of the Tall Cedars of Lebanon. The former, previously known as the Mystic Order of Veiled Prophets of the Enchanted Realm, was founded by a postmaster general of the United States, Thomas L. James. He emphasized that "although in many cases the government [of the Grotto] may be guided by Masonic usage as the most perfect system extant, it is to be strictly understood that in itself this is not a Masonic order and the degree is in no sense a Masonic degree." Several lodges in one city or area may support a local Grotto, which in turn sponsors dances, dinners, clambakes, outings, sports activities, and so on. The 27,000 Veiled Prophets sport fezzes, contribute to muscular dystrophy research, and generally pay less for their whoopla than do the Shriners. The Tall Cedars count 22,000 members and maintain Forests in only ten states. They have taken an interest in cerebral palsy clinics.

Although adoptive or "petticoat" Masonry has been popular in France since 1744, English and American Masons have been reluctant to establish ladies' auxiliaries to the lodges. The Order of the Eastern Star confers no Masonic secrets on the ladies, but only Master Masons and their female relatives may join the Order. The OES enrolls about 1,200,000 men and women.

Robert Morris composed the Eastern Star ritual in 1850, but it remained for Robert Macoy, a New York publisher of Masonic literature, to "sell" the auxiliary. By 1884 more than fifty thousand women and a few men had joined, and blacks who had obtained copies of the ritual launched a parallel order. Eastern Star meetings are usually held in a Masonic temple, and each OES chapter must include a Master Mason as patron. The Grand Lodge of Scotland, following the lead of the United Grand Lodge of England, forbids Masons to serve as patrons, so the OES barely exists in the British Isles.

Originally an advanced Eastern Star degree, the White Shrine of Jerusalem is limited to Christians and counts 58,000 members, about equally divided between men and women. Another former Eastern Star adjunct, the Order of Amaranth, numbers 45,000.

A popular boys' club, the Order of DeMolay, was founded in Kansas City in 1919 and has remained closely tied to the Scottish rite. DeMolay, last head of the suppressed Knights Templar, was executed in 1314. The order serves as a novitiate for Masonry and admits male relatives of Master Masons who are between the ages of fourteen and twenty-one. About half of the DeMolays eventually enter the Craft. Another youth organization, the Order of Builders, is sponsored by the Blue Lodges.

Masons also sponsor two societies for teenage girls. Job's Daughters was organized in 1921 for Christian girls between ages eleven and twenty who are related to Masons. They may continue as honorary members after they reach their twentieth birthday. The Order of Rainbow for Girls was founded a year later. Candidates must be daughters of Masonic or Eastern Star families or friends of such girls. Local assemblies operate under the supervision of a Masonic or Eastern Star organization.

Following the precedent of English Masonry, which forbids initiation of anyone in a military lodge below the rank of non-commissioned officer, membership in the National Sojourners is limited to active and retired commissioned and warrant officers in the armed forces of the United States. Chapters have been set up in every major military and naval post in the world. About ten thousand Masonic officers belong to the National Sojourners, but enlisted men who happen to be Masons may get together in informal Square and Compass clubs.

Once restricted to Master Masons, Acacia fraternity now admits Protestant college students who are Masons or sons or brothers of Masons or who are recommended by at least two Masons. The fraternity operates chapters on several dozen campuses. It began at the University of Michigan in 1904.

A sampling of the many other allied Masonic organizations might include: the Philalethes Society, which is interested in Masonic philosophy; the Order of the Golden Key, which seeks to establish a Masonic Center of Learning; the *Societas Rosicruciana in Civitatibus Foederatis*, which studies Masonic history and legends; the Society of Blue Friars, which honors Masonic authors; the Sword of Bunker Hill, which promotes patriotism; and High Twelve International, a Masonic luncheon club.[5]

[5] Further information can be found in *Allied Masonic Groups and Rites* (Silver Springs, Md.: Masonic Service Association, 1983).

Considering this panorama of Masonic organizations, we can imagine that a young man could enter the Order of DeMolay at fourteen, pledge Acacia fraternity at college, enter the Blue Lodge, serve his military obligation as an officer and affiliate with the National Sojourners, begin his Masonic climb through either or both the Scottish or York rites, don the fez of the Mystic Shrine, join his wife in the Order of the Eastern Star, and encourage his children to enter Job's Daughters, the Rainbow Girls, or the DeMolays.

Just as blacks are refused admittance to the white Blue Lodges and to the original Scottish and York rites, so they may not presume to apply for entry into any of these allied organizations on the basis of their Prince Hall affiliation. As a result, black Masons have set up their own rites, Eastern Star, Shrine, and the like. The black counterpart of the Shrine, known as the Ancient Egyptian Arabic Order Nobles of the Mystic Shrine, has attracted about fifty thousand Prince Hall Masons.

Thousands of Roman Catholic women and young people, by virtue of their relationship to Masons, qualify for membership in organizations such as the Eastern Star, Job's Daughters, and DeMolay. Although the possibility of scandal exists, the fact remains that these individuals do not swear Masonic oaths and are not Masons. The Catholic Church applies the general canonical principle that "favorable laws are to be interpreted broadly and odious laws are to be interpreted strictly." Since the purpose of these many allied groups is to foster Masonic principles that the Catholic Church sees as incompatible with her own, not many parish priests or bishops would be likely to encourage membership in such groups.

CHAPTER VIII

CATHOLIC ATTITUDES TOWARD THE LODGE

Eight Popes Have Condemned Masonry since 1738

No one could accuse the Catholic Church of disguising her antipathy to Freemasonry. Scarcely twenty years after the organization of modern Masonry in 1717, Pope Clement XII forbade membership in the lodge, and since then seven other popes have warned the faithful against the dangers of Masonic naturalism to the Christian faith.

The Roman Catholic Church prohibits her members from joining any form of Freemasonry, whether Grand Lodge, Grand Orient, Prince Hall, or co-Masonry. The official position is: "Catholics enrolled in Masonic associations are involved in serious sin and may not approach Holy Communion." This is taken from the declaration of the Sacred Congregation for the Doctrine of the Faith, dated November 26, 1983, as approved by Pope John Paul II.[1]

In previous chapters we have examined the chief reasons for the Church's severe attitude toward Masonry. Masonry constitutes a religion of naturalism that considers the basic Christian doctrines of the Trinity, the Incarnation, the Atonement, the necessity of baptism, and the role of the Church in the plan of salvation to be quite incidental. The

[1] See appendix.

lodge furthermore exacts a series of oaths from its candidates that cannot be called valid extrajudicial oaths; those who swear such oaths, agreeing to the most horrible self-mutilation in order to protect a few passwords and secret grips, are objectively guilty of either vain or rash swearing.

Pope Clement directed his bull *In Eminenti* (April 28, 1738) against Francis I, Grand Duke of Tuscany, who had sponsored Masonic lodges within his realm. The pontiff noted that the Masonic lodges were "content with a certain affection of natural virtue" and "are bound as well by a stringent oath sworn upon the Sacred Volume, as by the imposition of heavy penalties to conceal, under inviolable silence, what they secretly do in their meetings". Membership in a Masonic lodge by a Roman Catholic meant automatic excommunication.

Communications in 1738 did not encompass the daily newspapers, magazines, radio, TV, and motion pictures of today, and hence the Catholic world did not immediately know of the contents of the bull. According to ancient Church practice, a bull was not promulgated in a given diocese until it was posted and means were obtained to enforce it. Where Masonry was not yet a problem or where secular authorities prevailed upon individual bishops, the promulgation was delayed for many years. To add to the confusion, a bogus bull was circulated that asked the faithful to support the lodges whenever possible!

Consequently we find that some Catholics, particularly in Ireland, continued to join the lodge after the papal pronouncement. Some served as Worshipful Masters, and some lodges were composed entirely of Catholic priests and laymen. Even the Irish patriot Daniel O'Connell served as Master of Dublin Lodge No. 189 after his initiation in 1799. In 1837 he testified that he had renounced the lodge some years before.

Daniel Carroll, brother of the first American bishop, was active in Masonry, and apparently Bishop Carroll did not consider the papal ban applicable to this country until sometime after 1800. For example, the bishop discussed the various censures of the Holy See on the lodge question in a letter to a layman in 1794. He added, "I do not pretend that these decrees are received generally by the Church, or have full authority in this diocese." A convent of nuns in Nantes sent a Masonic apron to George Washington as a present. Masons laid the cornerstone for Saint Mary's Church, first Catholic church in Albany and first cathedral of that diocese. Catholics in the Louisiana Territory were likely to be members of the lodge, and Father Sedella, pastor of the New Orleans cathedral, was buried in Masonic regalia.

Clement's successor, Pope Benedict XIV, was equally adamant against the spreading secret societies, especially Freemasonry. He asked Maria Theresa, Empress of Austria, to disband the lodge in Vienna. Police almost arrested her husband, Francis I, when they raided the lodge room, but the Duke escaped through a back door. The captured Masons were detained for a day or two, but the lodge soon resumed underground activities. Benedict issued a second bull in 1751, reiterating the penalty of excommunication.

Pius VII (1821), Leo XII (1825), Pius VIII (1829), and Gregory XVI (1832) issued bulls against Freemasonry and the host of secret societies that were infesting the continent and thriving on intrigue, assassination, and subversion.

Pope Pius IX issued six bulls on Freemasonry between 1846 and 1873. His 1865 Allocution pointed out: "Among the numerous machinations and artifices by which the enemies of the Christian name have tried to attack the Church of God, and sought to shake it and besiege it by efforts superfluous in truth, must undoubtedly be reckoned that perverse society of men called Masonic, which, at first confined to darkness and obscurity, now comes into light for the common ruin of religion and human society."

Bishop John McGill of Richmond castigated the lodge in a pastoral letter published in 1884:

[Masonry] professes a great respect for religion, declaring that only men who respect religion can be members, and it amuses its members with a display of the Bible and certain prayers and religious terms, and while it inculcates the belief that the love of man and mere human virtues are all-sufficient and alone necessary, and in this manner it more effectually combats Christianity than can be done by the hosts of immoral and infidel writers who are openly laboring for its destruction. It is mighty in its agency, because it professes to dispose of the goods of the present life. It places its sword at the entrance of all the avenues of trade, business and professional life, and gives the accolade of patronage and success only to those who have learned its catechism and been initiated through the means of its supernatural signs. Its influence seriously affects all who refuse to enroll their names upon its list, upon all the fields of competition, and follows its members with the benefits of aid and protection upon the battlefields, in the prisons, before the tribunals of justice, and at the hustings. It throws the veil of concealment over its chief end and its internal administration by the requirements of a solemn oath of secrecy, and only makes itself known to the public by its festive processions with dazzling banners and regalia, and by its bountiful donations and timely assistance to the widows and orphans of deceased members.

The notorious Leo Taxil case illustrates the gullibility of some Catholics on the subject of Masonry. Although the hoax was exposed, some of the fantastic ideas about Masonry linger in Catholic folklore. Likewise, Masonic partisans point to the Taxil case as proof that the Church's case against the lodge is built on falsehoods and misunderstandings.

Taxil, a French anticlerical journalist, had written a sensational potboiler called *Secret Amours of Pius IX*, and he now saw another chance to get rich quickly and humiliate the Church he despised. He pretended conversion, recanted his atheist writings, and was received into the Church. He then published a series of books entitled *Complete Revelations of French Masonry*, in which he accused the lodges of demon worship, orgies, spiritualism, Black Masses, and so on. Masons were guilty of every crime from ritual murder to blasphemy, according to convert Taxil, who added that worship of Satan was the object of the higher degrees. He claimed that Charleston, S.C., then headquarters of the Scottish rite Southern Jurisdiction, was the fountainhead of diabolical Masonry, with Albert Pike as the Masonic pope. The high priestess of higher Masonry, a being with supernatural powers who was known as "Diana", allegedly rebelled when Pike commanded her to desecrate a Communion host. She also supposedly authored books on Masonry that were ghostwritten by Taxil.

Taxil was acclaimed as an outstanding authority on the inner workings of Masonry and was featured speaker at an anti-Masonic congress at Trent in 1896. The thousand delegates clamored for an appearance by the mysterious Diana, and Taxil promised to produce her in Paris on Easter Monday, 1897. Instead, the anti-Masonic mountebank astonished his admirers by announcing that his conversion twelve years earlier had been a pretense, Diana a myth, and his revelations pure fiction.

The naïveté of some Catholics in the Taxil case may serve as a wholesome lesson in examining Masonry. The Christian case against the lodge will never be served by checking intelligence and common sense at the door. During the course of research on this book, the author has heard tales of Masonic doings hardly less incredible than Taxil's famous fabrications. One clergyman solemnly described a death lottery in which all 33rd-degree Masons were said to participate. Every year one name is drawn, and supposedly the winner (loser) must agree to commit suicide in the following year for the greater glory of Freemasonry!

On the other hand, we cannot absolve the Masons for resorting to wild exaggeration and fables in seeking to discredit the papal condemnations. For years they circulated the canard that Popes Benedict XIV and Pius IX had themselves been initiated into the lodge. In a solemn allocution on April 20, 1849, Pius IX referred to the rumor about his Masonic initiation and denounced it as "the blackest of all calumnies".

One of the greatest modern popes, Leo XIII, was also one of Freemasonry's staunchest foes. Often called the pope of the workingman, Leo XIII issued his encyclical on Masonry, *Humanum Genus*, in 1884. This has embarrassed those Masons who argue that only political reactionaries among the hierarchy used the lodge as a red herring to divert the attention of the pope from needed social reforms. In his encyclical, the pope recalled:

> For as soon as the constitution and the spirit of the Masonic sect were clearly discovered by manifest signs of its actions, by cases investigated, by the publication of its laws, and of its rites and commentaries, with the addition often of the personal testimony of those who were in the secret, this Apostolic See denounced the sect of the Freemasons, and publicly declared its constitution as contrary to law and right, to be pernicious no less to Christendom

than to the State; and it forbade anyone to enter the society, under the penalties which the Church is wont to inflict upon exceptionally guilty persons.

He did not condemn all those who had joined the lodges, nor did he deny that Masonry also engaged in charitable works, but he insisted that "the Masonic federation is to be judged not so much by the things which it has done, or brought to completion, as by the sum of its pronounced opinions." He did accuse Masonry of attempting to "bring back after a lapse of eighteen centuries the manners and customs of the pagans". Leo XIII wrote: "As Our Predecessors have many times repeated, let no man think that he may for any reason whatsoever join the Masonic sect if he values his Catholic name and his eternal salvation as he ought to value them."

Said the head of the Southern Jurisdiction of the Scottish rite, "If, in other countries, Freemasonry has lost sight of the Ancient Landmarks, even tolerating communism and atheism, it is better to endure ten years of these evils than it would be to live a week under the devilish tyranny of the Inquisition and of the black soldiery of Loyola. Atheism is a dreary unbelief, but it at least does not persecute, torture, or roast men who believe there is a God." Tragically, history and international Communism have proved General Pike to be wrong. The General went out of his way to deny any basic distinction between American and Latin or Continental Masonry:

It is not when the powers of the Papacy are concentrated to crush the Freemasonry of the Latin Kingdoms and Republics of the world, that the Masons of the Ancient and Accepted Scottish Rite in the United States will, from any motive whatever, proclaim that they have no sympathy with the Masons of the Continent of Europe, or with those of Mexico or of the South American Republics. If these fall into errors of practice or indulge in extravagances of dogma, we will dissent and remonstrate; but we will not forget that the Freemasonry of our Rite and of the French Rite has always been the Apostle of Civil and Religious Liberty, and that the blood of Spanish and other Latin Freemasons has again and again glorified and sanctified the implements of torture, the scaffold and the stake, of the Papacy and the Inquisition.

Pope Leo XIII continued to warn against Masonic naturalism, and his 1892 letter to the Italian people sums up the attitude of the Roman Catholic Church then as well as now: "Let us remember that Christianity and Freemasonry are essentially irreconcilable, so that enrollment in one means separation from the other."

The Code of Canon Law issued by Benedict XV in 1917 reaffirmed the earlier Church practice that membership in a Masonic lodge meant automatic excommunication for a Roman Catholic. Such a "Catholic Mason" could not receive the sacraments or receive a Christian burial. A Freemason who wished to enter the Church had to sever all ties with the lodge. This remained the Church's position until publication of the new Code in 1983.

When the Second Vatican Council brought the Roman Catholic Church into the mainstream of the ecumenical movement, voices were heard to reexamine the long-standing prohibition against Masonic membership. Perhaps, some said, the Church's condemnations were rooted in musty political quarrels of the eighteenth and nineteenth centuries. Perhaps Freemasonry, at least in its Anglo-Saxon version, has changed and no longer poses a threat to Christian beliefs.

Between 1974 and 1980, the German Catholic bishops engaged in official dialogues with representatives of the

United Grand Lodges of Germany. The German Episcopal Conference assigned three tasks to the members of the Catholic dialogue group: "(1) to see if changes have taken place in Freemasonry, (2) to examine whether membership of the Catholic Church and simultaneously of Freemasonry is compatible, and (3) to prepare society with the media of social communication in the case of a positive reply to the two aforesaid points."[2]

The bishops concluded that Freemasonry had not changed and that "The thorough investigations of the rituals and essence of Freemasonry, as well as of its present-day, unchanged self-definition, show that: *Simultaneous membership of the Catholic Church and of Freemasonry is impossible*" (italics in the original).

Some of the points made by the Catholic participants in the official dialogue were: "The relativity of every truth represents the basis of Freemasonry. Just as the Mason rejects all faith in dogmas, he does not tolerate any dogma in his own Lodge." The Mason rejects all dogmas, and, the report notes, "This concept of truth is *incompatible with the Catholic one from the point of view of natural theology and of the theology of Revelation.*"

The report stated: "The religious conception of the Mason is relativistic: *all religions are competitive attempts* to explain the truth about God which, in the last analysis, is unattainable. Therefore, only the language of Masonic symbols, which is ambiguous and left to the subjective interpretation of the individual Mason, is adapted to this truth about God."

The German bishops gave close attention to the Masonic G.A.O.T.U., which is central in lodge rituals. They saw the Masonic concept as essentially Deistic rather than Theistic:

[2] *Amtsblatt des Erbistums Köln*, June 1980.

The "Great Architect of the Universe" is something neutral, not defined, and open to every interpretation. Every man can insert here his own concept of God: the Christian like the Muslim, the Confucian like the animist or the member of any religion. The "Architect of the Universe" is not for Masons a being in the sense of a personal God; so *any religious sentiment* is sufficient for them to recognize the "Architect of the Universe." This imagination of an "Architect of the Universe," sitting on a throne at a deistic distance, removes the foundation of the Catholics' concept of God and their response to God.[3]

That the Church has for centuries condemned Freemasonry and excommunicated Catholics who joined the lodge or refused baptism to those who declined to sever their lodge affiliations is clear. That the Church today considers Masonic membership serious enough to deny the Eucharist to "Catholic Masons" is also clear. What has created a pastoral problem in some U.S. dioceses is that for a period of some years membership by the laity in Masonic lodges seemed to be an option. From 1974 to 1981 and even beyond, an undetermined number of Catholic men joined the lodge, and many retain their membership. Articles in the Catholic press told readers that under certain circumstances such membership was now allowed. The general public, Catholic and non-Catholic, received the impression that the Church had softened her stand against membership in Freemasonry.

How did this misunderstanding come about, and how was it clarified?

Cardinal Franjo Seper, then prefect of the Sacred Congregation for the Doctrine of the Faith, sent a letter to Cardinal

[3] Ibid.

John Krol of Philadelphia, dated July 19, 1974, which concluded that "Canon 2335 regards only those Catholics who
join associations which plot against the Church." Even if it
were determined that a particular Masonic association did
not plot against the Church, membership was still forbidden
to clerics, religious, and members of secular institutes.

Presumably, the local ordinary was expected to conduct
an investigation to see whether a particular secret society in
his diocese was engaged in a plot against the Church. Cardinal Seper's letter made no reference to the traditional objections to Freemasonry, namely, its religious naturalism and its
oaths. Nor did the letter suggest a methodology by which a
bishop might conduct his investigation, in view of the fact
that the members of the lodge were sworn to secrecy. Some
bishops evidently conducted such investigations, or perhaps
decided they had no way of determining the character of a
particular secret society, and allowed Catholic men in their
dioceses to join the lodges. Other bishops denied requests to
join.

A clarification from the Congregation was published on
March 2, 1981. It referred to "erroneous and tendentious
interpretations" of the "confidential letter" of July 19, 1974.
The clarification affirmed that the present canonical discipline had not been modified in any way, that neither the
excommunication nor other penalties had been abrogated,
and that it was not the intention of the Congregation "to
remand to the bishops' conferences the making of public
pronouncements with a judgment of a general nature on the
nature of the Masonic associations, such as would imply the
derogation of the aforesaid norms."

Canon 2335 of the 1917 Code of Canon Law had stated:
"Those who join a Masonic sect or other societies of the
same sort, which plot against the Church or against legiti-

mate civil authority, incur excommunication." When the new Code of Canon Law was published, no mention was made of the traditional penalty of excommunication for Catholics who joined the Masonic lodge. Again the possibility of misunderstanding arose, because the general public was not aware that the number of offenses for which excommunication was applied had been reduced from thirty-seven to seven. The 1981 clarification had received little publicity. Cardinal Joseph Ratzinger then issued on November 26, 1983, the document of the Sacred Congregation for the Doctrine of the Faith that reaffirmed the historic position against Freemasonry. This statement had also been specifically approved by Pope John Paul II.[4]

In March 1985, *L'Osservatore Romano* published an article entitled "Irreconcilability between Christian Faith and Freemasonry".[5] The article noted that since Vatican II the Church has been urging collaboration between all men of good will, but it added that "becoming a member of Freemasonry decidedly exceeds this legitimate collaboration and has a much more important and final significance than this." The Vatican newspaper observed that, for the Catholic Christian,

> It is not possible to live his relationship with God in a twofold mode, that is, dividing it into a supraconfessional humanitarian form and an interior Christian form. He cannot cultivate relations of two types with God, nor express his relation with the Creator through symbolic forms of two types. That would be something completely different from that collaboration, which to him is obvious, with all those who are committed to doing good, even if beginning from different principles. On the one

[4] See appendix.
[5] *L'Osservatore Romano*, March 11, 1985.

hand, a Catholic Christian cannot at the same time share in the full communion of Christian brotherhood and, on the other, look upon his Christian brother, from the Masonic perspective, as an "outsider."

The article takes note of the various types of Masonic institutions, but "despite the diversity which may exist among Masonic obediences, in particular in their declared attitude toward the Church, the Apostolic See discerns some common principles in them which require the same evaluation by all ecclesiastical authorities." [6]

The United States Catholic bishops, through their Committee on Pastoral Research and Practices, authorized a study of Freemasonry, which was mailed as a confidential report to all bishops in this country on April 19, 1985. The thirty-eight-page report examined the history and principles of Masonry and came to the same conclusion as the German hierarchy: a man cannot be a Mason and a Roman Catholic at the same time. Somehow this report was leaked to the press and received wide dissemination by the secular and Catholic media.

Why the Church continues to condemn Freemasonry but no longer automatically excommunicates Catholic men who join the lodge was explained by Father John Connery, S.J., professor emeritus at Loyola University in Chicago and a consultant to the bishops' committee. "To understand the Church's position, you have to keep in mind that there is a difference between penal law and morality, between removing the punishment of excommunication for something and saying it is perfectly moral." The Jesuit theologian added: "The change in one doesn't change the other. Fornication or lying aren't punished by excommunication, but they're

[6] Ibid.

still wrong; they're still sinful. It's the same idea with Masonry—whether or not membership invokes excommunication, one simply can't possibly hold Catholic and Masonic principles at the same time."

The average druggist or shoe clerk in an American lodge can probably say with all honesty that he has never heard any anti-Catholicism in his lodge meeting. (A member of the Scottish rite, Southern Jurisdiction, would have to be unusually unobservant to make the same statement.) In any event, the Catholic Church does not make "anti-Catholicism" or "plotting against the Church" the reason for her condemnation of Freemasonry. If she did, it would be the same as saying that she was not concerned with the nature of the organization, its principles, or its teachings. By the same token the Church might allow membership by Catholics in organizations of Spiritualists, Theosophists, Rosicrucians, and Occultists as long as those groups did not plot against the Church. But the Church's historic stand has not been based primarily on whether the Masonic lodges are hostile or neutral or even friendly toward the Church but on the principles for which the lodge stands.

The problem of those hundreds, perhaps thousands, of Catholics who joined Masonic lodges in the U.S. from 1974 to about 1981 must be solved in a pastoral way. Many were assured by their pastors that such membership was allowed, so their good will should not be questioned.

Whatever the confusion in the late 1970s, no one should doubt that the Roman Catholic Church views Masonic membership by her sons as a grave matter, serious enough to deprive them of the Eucharist.

CHAPTER IX

PROTESTANT AND EASTERN ORTHODOX CRITICISM OF MASONRY

Majority of World's Christians Forswear the Lodge

Freemasonry would like to minimize the extent of Protestant and Eastern Orthodox opposition, so that the issue becomes the lodge versus the Vatican rather than the lodge versus Christianity. Yet tens of millions of non-Catholic Christians belong to churches that forbid or discourage lodge membership.

In the U.S. alone, more than twenty million Protestants and Eastern Orthodox belong to churches that take an anti-lodge stand. Worldwide, at least three out of four Christians belong to Catholic, Protestant, and Orthodox bodies that deny the compatibility of Christianity and Freemasonry.

For every Mason in the U.S., there are twenty Christian men who cannot join the lodge without turning their backs on their churches. And while membership in the United Methodist, Episcopal, Disciples of Christ, Presbyterian, and United Church of Christ denominations has been falling during the past three decades, membership has gone up dramatically in many religious groups that oppose the lodge: the Assemblies of God, Church of the Nazarene, most Pentecostal and fundamentalist churches, Jehovah's Witnesses, the Church of Jesus Christ of Latter-Day Saints (Mormons), and the Roman Catholic Church.

The *Lutheran Cyclopedia* explains why Masonry has had the success it has in England and the United States in attracting recruits from the Christian denominations:

> Due to the Wesleyan revival in England and the Great Awakening in the United States, with the influence of Protestantism still giving character to national life, Christianity, especially in the United States, was too strong to permit either Freemasonry or Oddfellowship to stress their deistic or anti-Church attitudes. While frankly anti-Christian in its French, German, and Italian branches, Freemasonry in England and the United States has always called itself a supporter of the morality and doctrine of the Protestant Church. Very few candidates realize that they are joining an organization which is essentially antagonistic to the Christian belief in the inspiration of the Bible and the divinity of Jesus Christ.[1]

In essentials, Protestants and Orthodox criticize the lodge for the same reasons as do Catholics. Furthermore, Protestants accuse the lodge of advocating salvation by good works rather than by faith alone. They are naturally distressed by the use in lodge services of mutilated Bible texts that delete the name of Jesus Christ, and they protest against being yoked with unbelievers in the fellowship of the lodge. The Protestant government of Holland banned Freemasonry in 1735 (three years before the first papal bull on the subject), and the governments of Lutheran Sweden and Calvinist Geneva followed suit in 1738. These bans were later lifted by secular governments.

Albert Pike's opinion of Protestantism was hardly more flattering than his views of Catholicism:

---

[1] *Lutheran Cyclopedia* (St. Louis, Mo.: Concordia Publishing House, 1954), p. 392.

Catholicism was a vital truth in its earliest ages, but it became obsolete, and Protestantism arose, flourished, and deteriorated. The doctrines of Zoroaster were the best which the ancient Persians were fitted to receive; those of Confucius were fitted for the Chinese; those of Mohammed for the idolatrous Arabs of his age. Each was Truth for the time. Each was a Gospel, preached by a Reformer; and if any men are so little fortunate as to remain content therewith, when others have attained a higher truth, it is their misfortune and not their fault. They are to be pitied for it, and not persecuted.[2]

Every Lutheran synod in the nation expresses opposition to oath-bound secret societies in its official statements; the nine million Lutherans in the U.S. form the second largest body of Christians to belong to anti-lodge churches, next to the sixty-one million Roman Catholics.

Lutheran opposition to Masonry has been spearheaded by the Lutheran Church-Missouri Synod (2,594,555 members) and the Wisconsin Evangelical Lutheran Synod (412,478).[3] The Missouri Synod's current handbook states, "The Synod has declared itself firmly opposed to all societies, lodges, and organizations of an unchristian or antichristian character." In practice, this has meant that no one may retain membership in the church or approach the communion table who has not renounced the lodge. The Wisconsin Synod takes a similar position. The Missouri Synod's Commission on Organizations "shall assist the pastors and the congregations of the Synod in fulfilling their commitment to witness publicly

[2] Albert Pike, *Morals and Dogma* (Charleston, S.C.: Supreme Council of the Thirty-third Degree for the Southern Jurisdiction of the United States, 1881), p. 38.

[3] All membership figures are taken from the *Yearbook of American and Canadian Churches* (Nashville: Abingdon Press, 1997).

and privately to the one and only Gospel set forth in the Holy Scriptures." The Commission conducts research and publishes its findings, which are available to Lutherans and others. The Evangelical Lutheran Church in America (5,200,000) forbids pastors from joining the lodge and discourages the laity from doing so.

These Lutheran bodies and others reflect the hostile attitude of continental Lutheranism toward the Masonic lodge. Every third Protestant in the world is a Lutheran, and the weight of Lutheran opposition to the Craft seriously undermines Masonic claims to Protestant approval.

The rapid growth of Pentecostal, Holiness, and fundamentalist denominations during the past three decades has been obvious to any observer of the American religious scene. Almost all of these churches take a negative attitude toward lodge membership. The Assemblies of God have grown fourfold in membership since 1957 and now report 2,387,982 members, making them the largest Pentecostal church. The position of the Assemblies of God is stated in Article VIII of the bylaws. These bylaws state in part that "all ministers affiliated with us should refrain from identifying themselves with any of the secret orders . . . and we advise any who may have identified themselves with such orders to sever their connections therewith." Further, "our ministers are requested to use their good influence among our lay members to dissuade them from such fraternal affiliations."

The smaller Pentecostal bodies, such as the United Pentecostal Church International (500,000) and the Pentecostal Holiness Church (113,000), also deny that a church member can maintain dual membership in the church and in the lodge.

A number of denominations grew out of the revival movement in nineteenth-century Methodism, and the largest of these is the Church of the Nazarene (601,900). This church's stand on Masonry has not wavered from its founding in 1908, when its first *Church Manual* stated: "We insist that our people abstain from membership in, or fellowship with, worldly, secret, or other oath-bound lodges and fraternities, inasmuch as the spirit and tendency of these societies are contrary to the principles of our holy religion." The current *Church Manual* continues this prohibition: "According to 33.3 of our *Manual*, one cannot be a member of the Church of the Nazarene while holding membership in an oath-bound secret order."

Another large Holiness denomination, the Christian and Missionary Alliance (307,316), does not have a written policy on lodge membership, but a church spokesman explains:

> While to the best of my knowledge we do not have a written statement, our official position is to discourage membership in the Masonic lodge. We do not from our international headquarters forbid membership, but we may have churches that have that in their local constitutions. They would have the freedom to do so. However, if anyone were to ask on the national level we would very, very strongly discourage membership in any type of secret or lodge societies.[4]

The attitude of these two denominations, the largest in the Holiness movement, is echoed in official statements by practically all of the many Holiness churches, including the several Churches of God.

When the Christian Reformed Church broke away from the parent Reformed Church in America in 1857, the issue of membership by Christians in the lodge was one of the main points of dispute. The Christian Reformed Church

[4] Letter dated June 13, 1986, to author from Dennis L Gorton of the Division of Church Ministries.

(206,789) has represented undiluted Calvinism and uncompromising hostility toward all secret societies since its founding. In its 1974 declaration, this church declared that "there is an irreconcilable conflict between the teachings and practices of the lodge and biblical Christianity, and that therefore simultaneous membership in the lodge and in the church of Jesus Christ is incompatible and contrary to Scripture."

The growing opposition to the lodge by Protestant churches has not gone unnoticed by Masons. In an article in the *Knight Templar*, the Associate Grand Prelate of the Grand Commandery of New Jersey discussed the traditional stance of the Roman Catholic, Lutheran, Christian Reformed, and other churches, but added:

> What is different today in the relationship between Freemasonry and organized religion is that Churches which have not traditionally been anti-Masonic are reexamining their understanding of Freemasonry. This factor, together with the reassertion of opposition from the traditional opponents, makes the relationship between certain organized religious groups in the United States and the various Grand Lodges and Masonic appendant bodies more problematic than it has been since the "Morgan era" (circa 1829), when Protestant Christian ministers were notable in their attacks on Freemasonry.

The author continued: "Both evangelicals and fundamentalists have become critical of Freemasonry in recent years."[5] He mentioned attacks on Masonry by television evangelists such as John Ankerberg.

The editor of *The Philalethes*, the journal devoted to Masonic research, discussed the spread of anti-lodge sentiment in an article entitled "The Power of Positive Hating". Wrote

[5] William H. Stemper, Jr., "An Analysis of Conflicts", *Knight Templar*, August 1986, p. 12.

Jerry Marsengill: "The mainline churches are rapidly losing members. The only churches which show a strong, continual growth pattern are the evangelical, charismatic, Pentecostal churches. . . . Many of these pentecostal churches are opposed to Freemasonry and to other fraternal organizations." The Masonic editor noted: "Not that the Masons have been entirely blameless in confronting these churches. Each time some Freemason states 'The Lodge is church enough for me', each time some Mason performing a Masonic funeral infringes on the perogatives [*sic*] of the church, more fuel is added to the fire." [6]

In recent years "born-again" Christians have also begun to ask awkward questions of their Masonic ministers in the mainline churches. One minister told the author he had been asked if he really thought most members of his congregation were "profanes", from whom he was bound by a solemn oath to conceal the spiritual wisdom he had received in the lodge. And if he refused to share this wisdom, was he being fair to his spiritual charges? If the wisdom was not all that secret, why did he take an oath on the Bible to conceal it? Another born-again member of his congregation asked him if he could honestly advise a fellow Christian to approach the lodge door as one "who has long been in darkness and seeks to be brought to light". The minister did not take a "demit" from his lodge, but he decided to cease active participation.

Several Protestant bodies oppose all oaths, even those asked in the courtroom. Naturally they would not consent to the use of an oath in a lodge initiation. They may also have other reasons for warning their members away from the lodge. In this category are the Quakers, Mennonites, and

[6] Jerry Marsengill, "The Power of Positive Hating", *The Philalethes*, August 1985, p. 17.

Brethren. A special committee of the Church of the Brethren (143,121) reported on the lodge problem in 1954 and decided:

> On the basis of information secured from representative pastors and laymen across the Brotherhood, the committee concludes that membership in secret societies involves only a small percentage of our members and creates a serious problem for only a few churches. Yet where such association with secret orders affects the loyalty of members to their church, we believe it constitutes enough of a problem that the church should again state its conviction that membership in secret, oath-bound orders represents a compromise with secular standards that is unworthy of a consecrated Christian.

The attitude of the estimated 175,000 Mennonites is reflected in the confession of faith adopted by the Mennonite Church (91,000), the largest of the dozen or so Mennonite bodies. In Article 17, the church declares: "We are opposed to membership in secret societies or lodges, because such membership would involve an unequal yoke with unbelievers, and because these organizations employ hierarchical titles, require oaths, stand for organized secrecy, and may offer salvation on grounds other than faith in the Lord Jesus Christ."

The 80,000 Amish reject membership in the Masonic lodges along with automobiles, radios, and television.

The various national organizations of Friends generally do not lay down requirements for members of local congregations, but it is quite unlikely that the estimated 123,000 Quakers would swear oaths in a Masonic lodge when they refuse to swear oaths in a court of law.

John Wesley, the founder of Methodism, once commented, "What an amazing banter on all mankind is Freemasonry." Today many of his spiritual heirs feel free to give allegiance to this banter. A significant number of United Methodist bishops, ministers, and laymen belong to Masonic lodges. They were probably surprised when the British Methodist Church in 1985 counseled church members to avoid the Masonic lodges.

The report on Freemasonry of the British Methodist Church noted that "For Christians, the secrecy practised by Freemasons poses a problem in that secrecy of any kind is destructive of fellowship. The Christian community is an open fellowship." The report observed: "The secrecy of Freemasonry is protected by the oaths sworn by members at different stages. These oaths are of an extravagant nature and include blood-curdling penalties for those who break their oaths. . . . The swearing of such oaths thus devalues the use of oaths or solemn words. . . . Certainly oaths should never contain extravagant words just to add colour, nor should they refer to penalties which cannot be enforced."

On the point of Masonry's religious orientation, the British Methodists commented:

> Freemasons are required to believe in a Supreme Being, sometimes called the Great Architect of the Universe. At various points in Masonic rituals, prayer is offered to this Being. Freemasonry claims to draw together those of different religions and Freemasons are required to respect one another's religious beliefs, and this is reflected in the prayers offered. However, the worship included in Masonic ritual seems to be an attenuated form unsatisfactory in any religious tradition. Christians must be concerned that the Supreme Being is not equated by all with God as Christians acknowledge Him, and prayer in Craft and Royal Arch Freemasonry is never offered in the name of Jesus Christ.

The report concludes, "Our guidance to the Methodist people is that Methodists should not become Freemasons."

Although the United Methodist Church raises no objection to dual church-lodge membership, two smaller Methodist bodies have long held to the position adopted by the British Methodists. The Wesleyan Church (115,867) has always rejected lodge or secret-society involvement on the part of its members. As long ago as 1845, this church declared, "We will on no account tolerate our ministers and members in joining secret oath-bound societies", and this remains the Wesleyan position today. The church's three main reasons for opposing the lodge are their secret operation, their quasi-religious nature, and their repugnant oaths. The *Book of Discipline* of the Free Methodist Church (74,707) states that the church insists that "those who are members of our church refrain from membership in all secret societies and that those who unite with the church resign from active membership in any lodge or secret order previously joined." The Free Methodist statement declares that these secret societies are "unitarian, not Christian; the religion is moralistic, not redemptive; and the ends are humanistic, not evangelical (Acts 4:12)".

Consternation spread through the Masonic hierarchy in 1992 when the Southern Baptist Convention voted to authorize a study of the lodge. With fifteen million members, the Southern Baptists make up the largest Protestant church in the U.S. The final report listed eight problem areas between Freemasonry and the SBC and concluded that "many tenets and teachings of Freemasonry are incompatible with Christianity and with Southern Baptist doctrine." Nevertheless, the SBC left it up to the conscience of the individual Baptist to decide whether to join or retain lodge membership.

Some smaller Baptist churches have taken a more emphatic stand. The Baptist Bible Fellowship claims 1,500,000 members, and its missions director, Dr. Carl Boonstra, wrote the author: "Baptist Bible Fellowship is a loose-knit fellowship of churches bound together around a missions program. Each church is answerable to its doctrine, standards, and policies. The churches that are associated together, to my knowledge, are all anti-freemasonry. We, as individual pastors and workers, have taken a stand against it." Likewise, the General Association of Regular Baptist Churches (136,380) opposes the lodge. Dr. Paul N. Tassell, National Representative, writes: "We are opposed to the false religions of secret lodges. We do not encourage membership in any secret order whatsoever."

Within the Church of England, a group of Anglo-Catholic priests and laymen raised a furor in 1951 with a proposal to investigate the religious basis of the Masonic order. King George VI, titular head of the Church at that time, and the Archbishop of Canterbury himself were both Masons. One of the leaders of the movement, Dr. Hubert Box, planned to ask for a committee to inquire "whether the theological implications of Freemasonry, as distinct from its benevolent activities, are compatible with the Christian faith as held by the Church". Dr. Box later wrote a penetrating analysis of the lodge entitled *The Nature of Freemasonry*. Another leader of the abortive effort, Walton Hannah, wrote *Darkness Visible*, which includes the complete Masonic Blue Lodge ritual as worked in England. A sequel, *Christian by Degrees*, examined the higher Masonic degrees, such as the Royal Arch and Rose Croix; its appendix listed by name seventeen Anglican bishops and more than five hundred priests who held higher degrees in the Craft. The motion to set up an investigating committee was naturally defeated in the Church Assembly.

The issue did not die, however, and the Church of England finally appointed a committee to study the question of Freemasonry and Christianity. The report was published in 1987.

The resolution to investigate the lodge was introduced by Roderick Clark, a free-lance journalist and member of the General Synod. In part, Clark said: "If we have here a sect offering its own salvation through secret knowledge to a privileged few, then this needs to be said clearly to the churchmen of our day." The resolution to study the question was approved overwhelmingly.

In the U.S., the Episcopal church has made no statement on membership in the lodge, and many Episcopalians are Freemasons. Individual priests and laity, especially in the Anglo-Catholic branch of the Episcopal church, continue to view the lodge with suspicion.

Fundamentalists in the United States generally avoid lodge affiliation, even when their churches are officially silent on the subject. The outstanding American evangelist Charles G. Finney renounced the lodge and wrote *The Character and Claims of Freemasonry* in 1869; it remains a persuasive exposé of the anti-Christian orientation of the lodge. Charles A. Blanchard, longtime president of Wheaton College in Illinois, described Masonry as "a heathen religion grafted onto the stump of a mechanic's guild". Evangelist Dwight L. Moody declared:

> I do not see how any Christian, most of all a Christian minister, can go into these secret lodges with unbelievers. They say they have more influence for good, but I say they can have more influence for good by staying out of them, and then reproving their evil deeds. Abraham had more influence for good in Sodom, although out of it, than Lot had in it. I would rather have ten church

members who were separated from the world, than a
thousand unseparated members. Come out of the Lodge.

Fundamentalist colleges such as Wheaton refuse to enroll
any student who does not agree to abstain from lodge membership as well as from liquor and tobacco.

General Booth, founder of the Salvation Army, circulated
a letter to all Army officers that included the following
passages:

> No language of mine could be too strong in condemning
> any officer's affiliation with any Society which shuts Him
> outside its Temples; and which in its religious ceremonies
> gives neither Him nor His name any place. . . . As for the
> future, the Army's views upon this matter will be made
> known to all who wish to become Officers and accep-
> tance of these views will be necessary before Candidates
> can be received for training, and further from this time it
> will be contrary to our regulations for any Officer to join
> such a Society.

The "Orders and Regulations for Officers of the Salvation
Army", issued by international headquarters in London and
applicable in all countries, states: "A person accepted for
officership may not be associated with any secret society,
neither may an officer join any such society." Soldiers in the
Salvation Army (446,000) are not forbidden to join a Masonic lodge, but neither are they likely candidates for initiation.

Most of the Eastern Orthodox churches are critical of the
lodge, although the largest Orthodox body in this country,
the Greek Archdiocese of North and South America, has
never issued an official opinion on Freemasonry. The bishops of the Church of Greece, meeting in 1933, called Freemasonry "a mystery-religion, quite different, separate, and

alien to the Christian faith . . . it possesses its own temples with altars, its own religious ceremonies, its own initiations, its own ceremonial ritual, its own hierarchical order and a definite discipline." The statement characterized Masonry as a "false and anti-Christian system".

No religious body has had as close ties with Masonry as the Church of Jesus Christ of Latter-Day Saints, or Mormons (4,711,500), and historically no two bodies have been more antagonistic than the Grand Lodge of Utah and the Mormon Church.[7] Joseph Smith, Jr., the founder of Mormonism, grew up in western New York state during the time of the anti-Masonic agitation, and anti-Masonic sentiments appear in the Book of Mormon. Yet by the time Smith had led his followers to Nauvoo, Illinois, he had mellowed on the subject and joined the Masonic lodge to which Brigham Young and other leading Mormon officials belonged. The Nauvoo lodge initiated as many as fifteen hundred Mormon Masons in a single year. Later both Smith and Young were expelled from the Masonic order, and the charters for the Nauvoo lodges were withdrawn by the Grand Lodge of Illinois.

After Joseph Smith, Jr., encouraged his people to destroy a Nauvoo newspaper critical of the church and its practice of polygamy, he was arrested and taken to jail in nearby Carthage. A mob of men with blackened faces stormed the jail, and many of the members of this vigilante party were later identified as Masons. Even as he was hit by volleys of gunfire, Smith gave the Masonic Grand Hailing Sign of Distress, but this did not deter his assassins. After Nauvoo, Brigham Young took no more interest in Masonry and discouraged any Latter-Day Saints from joining the lodge.

[7] See Marvin B. Hogan, *The Origin and Growth of Utah Masonry and Its Conflict with Mormonism* (Salt Lake City: Campus Graphics, 1978).

From the Masonic point of view, the prophet simply appropriated much of the lodge ritual for his own secret temple rites, especially the endowment ceremony. A study of Masonic and Mormon ritual confirms this assessment.[8] The Five Points of Fellowship, the oaths and penalties, the special grips or handshakes, the use of aprons, and the like lead the outside observer to conclude that Smith found his liturgical forms in the lodge room. Mormons can hardly deny the many parallels but insist that both the Mormon and the Masonic rituals came down from antiquity and that the Masonic rituals have been corrupted, while the Mormon rituals have retained their purity.

For decades the Grand Lodge of Utah excluded Mormon applicants simply by using the blackball. But in 1925 the Grand Lodge adopted a resolution that read in part:

> Whereas, the Church of Jesus Christ of Latter-Day Saints, commonly called the Mormon Church, is an organization, the teachings and regulations of which are incompatible with membership in the Masonic Fraternity, therefore: Be it resolved: That a member of the Church of Jesus Christ of Latter-Day Saints, commonly called the Mormon Church, is not eligible to become a member of any lodge F. & A.M., in this State, and membership in such Church shall be sufficient grounds for expulsion.

This religious test for initiation into Freemasonry was unique among U.S. Grand Lodges and created problems for the Grand Lodge of Utah. It was finally repealed in 1984.

The Mormon Church has generally ignored the Masonic lodge, and the only Mormons likely to seek Masonic affiliation are nominal church members. Certainly advancement

---

[8] For a description of Mormon temple rites, see William J. Whalen, *The Latter-Day Saints in the Modern Day World*, rev. ed. (South Bend, Ind.: University of Notre Dame Press, 1967), chap. 11.

in the Mormon priesthood would be unlikely for anyone involved with the lodge. Don LeFevre, manager of press relations for the Mormon Church, wrote the author:

The Church strongly advises its members to refrain from joining any organization that is secret or that is antagonistic toward the Church or would cause them to lose interest in Church activities or cause them to violate Church standards or which would interfere with their performance of Church duties. I repeat, this is a general guideline. Individual members considering affiliation with any type of organization are encouraged to apply these factors to their decision-making process [dated May 21, 1986].

We do not have the space to examine the official positions of all the denominations that condemn the lodge. In 1996 the Church of God (Anderson, Indiana; 214,000) declared: "Freemasonry is a Christless religion that omits the name of Jesus Christ and has a false view of God and the nature of His salvation." A decade earlier the Presbyterian Church in America (239,000) said that "joining the Masons requires actions and vows out of accord with scripture." The Orthodox Presbyterian Church and the Reformed Presbyterian Church hold similar views.

Two religious bodies that are among the fastest growing in this country have also taken strong anti-lodge stands: the Seventh-Day Adventist Church (790,731) and Jehovah's Witnesses (966,243).

Since so many Christian churches—Catholic, Protestant, and Eastern Orthodox—have taken a positive stand against Masonry, we may ask why all Christian denominations have not taken a similar stand. Several reasons explain why some churches tolerate or even encourage lodge membership.

First, some Protestant churches may see no conflict between their interpretation of Christianity as primarily an ethical system and the religious naturalism of the lodge. Those churches that emphasize the authority of the Bible and lay stress on theology, creeds, and confessions are the ones most likely to frown on lodge membership. Among the churches influenced the most by rationalism, the Masonic credo, which demands belief in a Supreme Being and in the immortality of the soul, may even be *too* dogmatic; the Unitarian Universalist Church and some others consider these beliefs dogmatic and beyond what they ask of church members.

Second, many Protestant denominations are organized along congregational lines and take no stand on theological issues, which must be left to the congregations themselves. This includes any position on secret societies. The Baptist churches, for example, comprise the largest Protestant family in the U.S., but the national bodies would never take a stand, pro or con, on Masonry since they have no authority over the local congregations. Individual pastors and congregations may have reservations about lodge membership, and some Baptist preachers are vocally anti-Masonic.

Third, some denominations seem to be under the impression that the rituals and teachings of Masonry are really secret and that consequently no outside agency can successfully investigate the lodge. Of course, anyone who has done research in this area can testify that authentic lodge rituals are easily procured and that extensive libraries of materials are available to anyone interested in research. Churches that have witnessed against the lodge for many decades, such as the Lutheran Church–Missouri Synod, have compiled materials on Freemasonry that they regularly share with other Christians.

Fourth and finally, we must conclude that some Protestant churches have so many Masonic ministers, benefactors, and laymen that they will probably never take a close look at the compatibility of the lodge and biblical Christianity. A genuine investigation of the lodge question by the United Methodist, Presbyterian, or Episcopal churches is unlikely. Again, individual pastors in these denominations may entertain serious reservations about Masonic naturalism and the oaths, may decline suggestions that they join the lodge, and may discourage active church members from joining if they seek their counsel in this matter. The head of a medium-sized denomination wrote the author: "I suspect most of the ministry of the —— Church would be opposed to Freemasonry, but there is a hesitancy to press the issue too sharply, since we could possibly split the Church over it."

Some Christians get advice from the clergy that ignores the serious objections to Masonry and puts the matter on a "boys will be boys" level. For example, some years ago a distraught wife wrote Dr. Norman Vincent Peale to say that her husband had joined a lodge and that she now felt she had lost his confidence and had been cut out of his life. She declared she had never believed in secret organizations. Dr. Peale replied:

> As a fraternal-organization member, I can assure you that you should be glad of your husband's membership. Such lodges teach the highest standards of conduct and are creative influences. There is no "secret" that isn't good. Since most fraternal orders are founded on the Bible, the "secrets" are all there. Relax and have a sense of humor. Don't you know that all men are boys and like a gang, especially if there are jokes and passwords and such paraphernalia? Don't let jealousy and insecurity become a barrier between your husband and you. Why not join the women's auxiliary such fraternal orders usually have, and have a few "sisters" and "secrets" yourself? You'll have lots of fun.[9]

[9] *Look*, April 1, 1958, p. 60.

Where Protestant denominations with Masonic sympathies predominate in a community, such as in the South or in many rural areas, the local Masonic lodge often takes on the appearance of an interfaith men's fellowship. The vigorous opposition of other Protestants and of Orthodox and Catholic Christians is ignored or unknown. This situation is confined to England and the United States; where Grand Orients represent Masonry, the conflict between lodge and church for the Christian's loyalty is unknown. "The problem of a Freemason who is also a member of a Christian Church, be it Catholic, Orthodox or Protestant, does not really arise in France", writes Marius Lepage.[10]

What is significant is that the great majority of the world's Christians see the lodge as the cultic expression of naturalism and as such a rival to the Christian faith. Furthermore, as Hannah points out, "No Church that has seriously investigated the religious teachings and implications of Freemasonry has ever yet failed to condemn it."[11] It becomes Masonry's public-relations task to squelch any moves for such an investigation on the part of other Protestant denominations and to belittle the considerable opposition to the lodge by non-Catholic Christians.

---

[10] *Le Symbolisme*, June–July 1953.
[11] Walton Hannah, *Darkness Visible* (London: Augustine Press, 1952), p. 78.

CHAPTER X

MASONRY IN OTHER COUNTRIES

World Freemasonry Overwhelmingly English-Speaking

Probably no more than one Mason out of twenty received his initiation in a lodge that uses a language other than English. Outside of the U.S., the great majority of Freemasons live in England, Scotland, Canada, Australia, and New Zealand. There are more Masons in a single state such as Kentucky or Georgia than in all the Grand Lodges and Grand Orients of continental Europe. Yet these Grand Orients rally the anticlerical minorities in their respective nations and historically have demonstrated bitter hostility toward the Christian churches.

Since these Grand Orients in countries such as France and Belgium do not require profession of belief in the G.A.O.T.U. or the immortality of the soul or use the V.S.L. in administering their Masonic obligations, they are considered heretics by Anglo-Saxon Masons.

Masonic claims and anti-Masonic indictments to the contrary, the Masonic order does not form one worldwide fraternity. Masonry embraces "orthodox" Masons recognized by the Grand Lodge of England, heretical Masons in Grand Orients that have discarded what the majority believe to be essential landmarks, black Masons in Prince Hall lodges, Christian Masonic lodges in the Scandinavian countries, rival Grand Orients in some European and Latin American nations, and small groups of co-Masons who admit both men and women to membership. Individual Masons may express sympathy for irregular bodies, but officially their Grand Lodges withhold fraternal relations and visiting privileges from these atheistic Grand Orients, Prince Hall lodges, and schismatic lodges of various types.

Regular Masons are organized in some one hundred independent jurisdictions, of which fifty-two are American and nine Canadian. Most lodges outside the United States are grouped in national Grand Lodges; American lodges are organized in state Grand Lodges, and no serious proposals for a central Grand Lodge of the United States have been put forth since the time of Washington. Grand Orients usually claim jurisdiction over both Blue Lodge and "higher degrees".

We have postponed discussion of non-American Masonry for several reasons. First, we wanted to demonstrate that the Christian case against the lodge was not predicated on a condemnation of the openly atheistic Grand Orients but on the naturalism and oaths of Anglo-Saxon Masonry. Second, we believe that American readers may be less interested in the machinations of foreign Masons than in the status of the Craft in this country. Third, American Masonry constitutes by far the largest body of Masons in the world.

English Masonry has cultivated good relations with the crown, the aristocracy, and the Established Church and has scrupulously observed the Masonic landmark against political and religious debate within the lodge. Of course, the present queen may not enter into the mysteries of the lodge, but her father, George VI, was an active Mason, and her husband, the Duke of Edinburgh, was initiated in 1952. By this triple alliance of crown, church, and lodge, the English were able to harness the revolutionary energy of the Masonic lodges that was typically directed against Church and State on the continent.

Prince Charles has declined to join the Masonic lodge and is reported to have told friends when he reached age twenty-one: "No. I do not want to join any secret society." If he persists in his refusal, he will be the first English king in many decades to remain among the "profane". Both his favorite uncle, Lord Mountbatten, and the Queen Mother, his grandmother, disapproved of the lodge and may have influenced his decision.

Such American innovations as the Shrine, DeMolay, and Job's Daughters are unknown in English Masonry, which has been most careful to maintain its dignity and decorum. The blatant anti-Catholicism of the Scottish rite's Southern Jurisdiction, the silly antics of the Shriners, and the gruesome skull libations of the American Knights Templar would not be tolerated by English Masons.

In 1730, eight years before the papal condemnation of Masonry, the Duke of Norfolk, a Roman Catholic, was installed as Grand Master of the English lodge. In 1874 Grand Master the Marquess of Ripon shocked English Freemasonry by resigning from the supreme post of the Craft to enter the Catholic Church. He had served as Grand Master for four years. His successor was the playboy Prince of Wales, who resigned his Grand Mastership in 1901 to become Edward VII. Edward's brother, the Duke of Connaught, served as Grand Master for thirty-eight years.

Some six hundred thousand Masons belong to the eight thousand recognized lodges in England and Wales. Many of these lodges are quite small; London alone has twelve hundred lodges. An estimated one hundred thousand men belong to Scottish lodges and sixty thousand to those in Ireland. At the end of the eighteenth century the Craft counted more lodges in Ireland than in England; the eventual promulgation of the papal bulls against Masonry depleted the Irish lodges. Traces of the Christian heritage of the Craft may still be found in Irish workings, and the name of Christ may be used in lodge prayers when its use will not offend anyone present. Irish Catholic critics of the lodge have seen Masonry as an ally of British and Protestant landlords and have too often been inclined to exaggerate the role of Masonry in world affairs.

Even small English towns of four or five thousand support two or three Masonic lodges of varying social prestige. The oldest or "snob" lodge will enroll the best people of the community. The largest cities, such as London, Birmingham, and Liverpool, include a number of "class" lodges that are open to members of certain professions. For example, the Mendelssohn Lodge in London enrolls only musicians. Most exclusive of these lodges is the Guildhall Lodge for Aldermen only.

Stephen Knight observes: "Far from being revolutionary, there is no organization more reactionary, more Establishment-based, than British Freemasonry. Its members derive benefit from the Brotherhood only so long as the status quo is maintained."[1]

In 1984 the twenty-seven thousand police officers in London were advised not to join the Masonic lodge or, if they were members, to resign. This action came after a thorough investigation into improper conduct within the police department. The Assistant Chief Police Commander stated that police officers could have their impartiality compromised because of obligations required of Masons toward their brother Masons.[2]

[1] Stephen Knight, *The Brotherhood: The Secret World of Freemasons* (New York: Stein and Day, 1984), p. 3.

[2] *Dutch Daily N.R.C.*, September 6, 1984.

From England the Craft spread to France with the chartering of the lodge *Amitié et Fraternité* at Dunkirk in 1721. Not content with the three degrees of the Blue Lodge, the French Masonic enthusiasts invented scores of higher degrees, most of which have become museum pieces. Occultism infiltrated French Masonry to a greater degree than it did in the parent body, and the Grand Orient drifted from deism to atheism.

Both opponents and partisans of Freemasonry have claimed that the lodges played a larger role in the French Revolution than history indicates. Most French Masons were royalists who would not be expected to encourage the extreme republicanism of the Revolution. In 1793 the Grand Master of the Grand Orient, Philippe-Egalité, resigned his position, and the lodges deteriorated for several years. A famous Catholic lay leader, Comte de Maistre, was proud to be an Ultramontane and a Freemason.

Napoleon, whose Masonic status is uncertain, sought to control the lodges as well as the Church. He made his brother Joseph Grand Master of the Grand Orient in 1805. Gradually the aristocrats took less interest in the lodge, and their places were taken by merchants, bureaucrats, journalists, and lawyers. Napoleon III nominated Marshall Magnan as Grand Master, even though his nominee was not a Mason and had to hustle through all thirty-three degrees in a single day.

When in 1877 the Grand Orient removed from its Constitutions the requirement of belief in the Supreme Architect and discontinued the use of the V.S.L. in administering the oath, the Grand Lodges of the world ostracized the French lodges as "heretical". The Grand Orient's action was designed to accommodate a number of Positivists who wished to enter the fraternity without subscribing to a belief in a Supreme Being.

From the fall of the MacMahon government in 1877 until World War II, Masons held the reins of the French government. Religious orders were disbanded and expelled, and Church schools were forced to close. Typical of the sentiments of the French lodge were those of Senator Delpech given at a Masonic banquet in 1902:

> The triumph of the Galilean has lasted twenty centuries; he is dying in his turn. The mysterious voice which once in the mountains of Epirus announced the death of Pan, today announces the death of the deceiver God who had promised an era of justice and peace to those who should believe in him. The illusion has lasted very long; the lying God in his turn disappears; he goes to rejoin in the dust of ages the other divinities of India, Egypt, Greece, and Rome, who saw so many deluded creatures throw themselves at the foot of their altars. Freemasons, we are pleased to state that we are not unconcerned with this ruin of false prophets. The Roman Church, founded on the Galilean myth, began to decline rapidly on the day when the Masonic association was constituted. From the political point of view Freemasons have often varied. But in all times Freemasonry has stood firm on this principle: war on all superstitions, war on all fanaticism.

During this same period of Masonic ascendency in France the notorious *affaire des fiches* was exposed. The Grand Orient kept index cards on each army officer indicating if the officer attended Mass, allowed other members of his family to practice their religion, sent his children to religious instruction, encouraged religion among his troops, and so on. These cards were forwarded to the War Department, and those who were guilty of such Christian practices were ineligible for promotion and assigned to the least desirable posts.

Over eighteen thousand officers were thus blacklisted by the Grand Orient between 1901 and 1904 before photographic evidence was produced to expose the conspiracy. The revelation demoralized the French army and revealed the power of the Masonic minority in that nation.

A rival Masonic body, the Grand Loge Nationale, was established in Paris in 1914 by dissidents who wished to restore the use of the V.S.L. and the invocation to the Grand Architect. This new Grand Lodge won recognition from the English lodge and has since had modest success. A third body, the Grand Lodge of France, was established in 1895. It does require the V.S.L. on its altars and asks candidates to affirm belief in the Supreme Architect. But because it also allows visitation by Grand Orient Masons, few Grand Lodges in the U.S. have extended recognition. With 27,000 members, the Grand Orient is the largest of the three Masonic bodies; the Grand Lodge has 22,000, and the National Grand Lodge of France reports 13,000. Masonry no longer attracts the militant anticlerical, who now finds other outlets for expressing his hatred of Christianity. The domination of French political life by Masons seems to be over.

In France, as in other European nations, Freemasonry has always been an elite movement rather than the mass movement the Craft has become in the U.S. and England. A Master Mason in Chicago can advance to the 32nd degree over a weekend; in Paris or Rome the path to the same degree can take as long as fifteen years and involves study, careful scrutiny, examinations, and demonstrated devotion to the principles of Masonry.

The German lodges were barely tolerated by orthodox Lutherans, condemned by Catholics, disbanded by the Nazis, scorned by the Communists and Socialists, and usually closed to Jews. The "Humanitarian" lodges in Hamburg and Frankfurt would admit a few Jews, but the "Christian" lodges of Prussia and Berlin were traditionally anti-Semitic.

Hamburg was the site of the first German lodge in 1737, and we have seen that Frederick the Great dabbled in the Craft at one stage in his career. Goethe, Mozart, Haydn, and Fichte were among the Masonic initiates in the eighteenth century, and most of the Prussian officers and many members of the Hohenzollern dynasty joined in the nineteenth century. As many as eight independent Grand Lodges were functioning in Germany at one time. Hitler outlawed the lodge, confiscated its temples and paraphernalia, and practically obliterated all traces of Masonry in the Third Reich. Today about twenty thousand German Masons are grouped in 250 lodges. American military officers have been instrumental in the postwar Masonic revival in Germany.

The patronage of royalty has given Scandinavian Masonry a prestige it has not enjoyed elsewhere except in England. The sovereigns are hereditary Grand Masters of these lodges, which enroll a much more select membership than in either England or America. For example, there are only about ten thousand Masons in Norway, twenty-three thousand in Sweden, and several hundred in Finland. Scandinavian Masonry is barely recognizable, combining the York rite with Christian and Swedenborgian elements.

The Belgian lodge has become so deeply involved in politics that it has been disowned by most other branches of the Craft. The first Belgian lodge was opened in 1770 and gained independence from French control in 1814. Brussels University, the only university in Europe not founded by Church or State, was established by Freemasons in 1834 as a rival to the Catholic University of Louvain. Naturally, the Catholic royal family does not patronize the lodge.

The Dutch Grand Orient was formed in 1758 and maintains cordial relations with Grand Lodges in England and America. There are only six thousand Blue Lodge Masons in the Netherlands, and five hundred of these have also joined the Scottish rite. No one petitions to join the Scottish rite in Holland; Blue Lodge members are observed, tested, and eventually invited to join.

Joseph Bonaparte encouraged the spread of the lodge in Spain, and the aggressively political and anticlerical Spanish lodges contributed to Spanish unrest for decades. English Masons were unable to recognize the Spanish Grand Orient because of various irregularities.

In neighboring Portugal, Masonic politicians gained control of the nation in 1910 and set up a republic with the following Constitutional provisions:

> Ministers of religion shall have no part in the parochial lay corporations or associations in charge of temporal affairs. A minister of religion who criticizes or attacks any of the acts of a public authority or the form of government or the laws of the Republic or any of the provisions of the present law will be punishable by law. Church property shall belong to the State, but shall be loaned to the Church. The wearing of the clerical habit outside of the churches and ceremonies is prohibited. It is also prohibited to publish in any way by word or deed, any bulls, decrees, or communications from the Roman Curia, or prelates, or others, without explicit permission from the civil authorities. The State will have charge of naming and approving the professors in ecclesiastical seminaries for the training of priests and will determine the textbooks and courses of study therein. No Jesuits or other monastic orders or religious congregations shall be admitted into Portuguese territory. All Jesuits, whether alien, naturalized citizens, or natives, are expelled, and all their real or personal property is confiscated. As for the members of other

religious orders, if they are aliens or naturalized citizens, they are likewise to be expelled, and if they are natives, they must return to secular life, or at least may not live in community, and shall not be allowed to exercise the teaching profession or intervene in any way in education.

Over the years most of these restrictions have been rescinded in this overwhelmingly Catholic nation. When Dr. Antonio de Oliveira Salazar became prime minister in 1933, he took steps to deny legal status to the Masonic order and similar secret societies.

Carried to Italy in 1733, the Masonic order was first known there as the "Company of the Trowel". With the rise of the revolutionary Carbonari and Young Italy movements between 1814 and 1860, the lodges were eclipsed. Garibaldi formed a Grand Orient in Palermo in 1860, and at Mazzini's funeral in 1872 Masonic banners were seen on the streets of Rome. Although Mussolini included a number of Masons in his first government, he soon turned on the lodge and extinguished Freemasonry in fascist Italy. The dictator ordered all Masonic emblems removed from Garibaldi monuments and replaced with fasces and axes.

After World War II, U.S. military personnel and such Italo-American Masons as Mayor Fiorello LaGuardia of New York helped revive Italian Freemasonry. The main Grand Orient and two smaller bodies managed to attract about fifteen thousand members in some five hundred lodges, but not much was heard from Italian Freemasonry until 1981, when the exposure of an amazing Masonic conspiracy toppled the government of Premier Arnaldo Forlani. It is known as the P2 case.

This secret Masonic organization, *Propaganda Due*, or P2, was the means by which a millionaire businessman, Licio Gelli, hoped to subvert the democratic government of his country and reestablish a fascist state. The Italian constitution (Article 18) forbids secret societies, but most Masonic lodges comply with the law by agreeing to submit lists of members to government officials. P2 did not meet this requirement.

Gelli was a high-ranking Fascist during the war and a die-hard Nazi sympathizer. He had fought with Franco's Blackshirts during the Spanish Civil War, and after World War II he lived for some years in Argentina and boasted of his friendship with dictator Juan Perón. Gelli joined the Masonic lodge in 1962.

Gelli obtained Grand Orient approval to found P2 and eventually enrolled almost a thousand members of the Italian establishment. All members swore loyalty to Gelli, the Venerable Grand Master. The P2 lodge never met as a body, and lodge brothers knew only members of their own cells, of which there were seventeen; probably only Gelli himself knew the identity of the entire lodge.

Getting wind of the political activities of P2, the Grand Orient withdrew recognition in 1974, but Gelli managed to reestablish his lodge within two months. In July 1976 the Grand Orient placed P2 under "indefinite suspension". About the same time the Vatican felt obliged to restate its opposition to all forms of Masonry, since some P2 members had been persuaded to join on the grounds that the Catholic Church no longer condemned such affiliation.

In March 1981 Italian investigators raided Gelli's villa and discovered the membership roster of P2, along with hundreds of secret and sensitive state documents. The Italian people were astounded to find out that P2 Masons included three members of the cabinet; forty-three members of parliament; thirty generals and eight admirals among the 183 officers of the army, navy, and air force; the editor of Italy's leading newspaper, *Il Corriere della Sera*; fifty-eight university professors; the directors of the three top intelligence services; lawyers, bankers, and many others—953 in all. All had sworn allegiance to Gelli, and all were in violation of Italian law as members of a secret society.

As one prosecutor put it, "Lodge Propaganda Due is a secret sect that has combined business and politics with the intention of destroying the country's constitutional order." A magistrate called P2 "a right-wing state-within-a-state". The lodge was implicated in dozens of cases of tax fraud, espionage, illegal currency dealings, and terrorist attacks.

Besides Gelli, a number of other Italian Masons soon became familiar to readers of U.S. newspapers. Roberto Calvi, the president of Banco Ambrosiano, although a Freemason, served as a financial adviser to the Vatican. His bank collapsed, and he was said to have incriminating evidence about many of his fellow P2 brothers. On June 18, 1982, his body was found hanging by the neck from the scaffolding under Blackfriars Bridge in London. His pockets were filled with chunks of masonry, and perhaps it is only a coincidence that the traditional symbol of Italian Freemasonry is the figure of a Blackfriar. Whether his death was murder or suicide has not been resolved, but many think it unlikely that a middle-aged man suffering from vertigo would travel four miles from his London hotel, clamber up the scaffolding, and hang himself.

Another prominent Italian Freemason and Calvi's mentor, Michele Sindona, extended his financial dealings to the U.S. and gained control of the Franklin National Bank.[3] In the late 1950s he had met Msgr. Giovanni Montini, archbishop of Milan, and had contributed a large gift to a Church home for the aged. When Archbishop Montini

[3] For more on Sindona, see Nick Tosches, *Power on Earth: Michele Sindona's Explosive Story* (New York: Arbor House, 1986).

became Pope Paul VI, he asked Sindona to help manage the Vatican's finances. Sindona was often called "God's Banker". In the end the financial machinations of Sindona and Calvi cost the Vatican more than $240 million.[4]

When Sindona's Franklin National Bank collapsed in 1974, it was the worst banking default in U.S. history, and Sindona faced an assortment of federal charges. Just before his trial in August 1979, Sindona skipped bail in a fake kidnapping arranged by his fellow Masons. When he re-appeared, he was tried and convicted of sixty-eight counts of fraud, perjury, and misappropriation of bank funds. Sindona was serving a twenty-five-year prison term when he was extradited to Italy and convicted of the murder of a lawyer. He drank coffee laced with cyanide. A magistrate in Milan ruled that Sindona had killed himself by swallowing enough poison "to kill a horse". Judge Antonio de Donno said, "There is no penal action regarding the death of Michele Sindona since it was suicide."

Gelli fled the country after the P2 scandal and was wanted on a variety of charges, including espionage and arms deal-ing. He was captured in Switzerland but escaped from a Swiss jail just before his expected extradition to Italy. He has not surfaced, but some think his escape is another piece of evidence that elements of the P2 Masonic lodge still operate.

The Grand Orient of Italy did try to dissociate itself from P2, but the case illustrates the potential for mischief that secret societies pose in a democratic state. The fact remains that all of the P2 members were Freemasons bound by Ma-sonic oaths and that the purpose of the lodge was to subvert the legitimate government, enrich the brethren, and set up an authoritarian state along neofascist lines.

[4] See Penny Lernoux, *In Banks We Trust* (New York, Anchor Press/ Doubleday, 1984), p. 193.

Strong opposition by the Greek Orthodox Church handicapped the growth of the Craft in Greece. The fifty or so lodges were destroyed during World War II, but efforts at revival have been made with American assistance. King George, a member of the Church of Greece, defied the pronouncements of the bishops by becoming a Mason during his exile in England.

Before the rise of Kemal Ataturk, Turkey was to secret societies what Los Angeles has been to religious cults. Ataturk used his Masonic membership to advantage in his seizure of power and then denounced the lodge and closed its Turkish temples.

Emperor Peter III served as Grand Master of the Russian lodge, which was organized in Saint Petersburg in 1771. The Russian Orthodox Church expressed its disapproval, and Alexander I closed the lodge in 1822. Pierre, in Tolstoy's monumental *War and Peace*, joins this Saint Petersburg lodge and later discusses his beliefs with the cynical Prince Andrew: "I myself thought like that, and do you know what saved me? Freemasonry. No, don't smile, Freemasonry is not a religious ceremonial sect, as I thought it was. Freemasonry is the best expression of the best, the eternal aspects of humanity." International Communism scorned the bourgeois pretensions of Masonry; the lodge was outlawed in Soviet Russia in 1922, and postwar revivals in such satellites as East Germany were nipped in the bud.

A resolution of the fourth Congress of the Communist International expressed the attitude of the Bolsheviks toward the lodge:

> It is absolutely necessary that the leading elements of the Party should close all channels which lead to the middle classes and should therefore bring about a definite breach with Freemasonry. The chasm which divides the proletariat

from the middle classes must be clearly brought to the consciousness of the Communist Party. A small fraction of the leading elements of the Party wished to bridge this chasm and to avail themselves of the masonic Lodges. Freemasonry is a most dishonest and infamous swindle of the proletariat by the radically inclined section of the middle classes. We regard it as our duty to oppose it to the uttermost.

Communist opposition to bourgeois Masonry did not rule out the use of the Masonic lodges as a cover for KGB operations. Stephen Knight attempted to prove that the KGB had instructed its operatives to infiltrate English lodges so that its agents could enjoy the preferential treatment one Mason affords another.

The British exported Freemasonry to India, where it captured the fancy of some of the native princes and the wealthy Parsees. Rudyard Kipling was initiated at Lahore in 1886, with a Hindu as Worshipful Master; the other lodge officers included a Muslim, an English Christian, and a Jew. The poet later wrote:

My Mother Lodge

Outside, "Sergeant! Sir! Salute! Salaam!"
Inside—"Brother!" and it doesn't do no 'arm,
We met upon the level an' we parted on the square,
An' I was Junior Deacon in my Mother-Lodge out there!
We 'adn't good regalia,
An' our Lodge was old and bare,
But we knew the Ancient Landmarks,
An' we kept 'em to a hair;
An' lookin' on it backwards
It often strikes me thus,
There ain't such things as infidels
Excep', per'aps, it's us.

Turning to the Western hemisphere, we find about 246,000 Canadian Masons in nine Grand Lodges and small hard cores of Masons in the Central and South American countries.

Mexican Masonry presents a jumbled picture of schisms and feuds. Two rival Grand Lodges claim a combined membership of twelve hundred Masons. Novelist Evelyn Waugh describes the role of the lodge in recent Mexican history:

> The first instrument of this policy was Joel Poinsett, who came to Mexico at the establishment of its independence, first as United States agent, later as accredited minister; the means he chose, perhaps the only efficacious means he could have chosen, was the establishment of a rival secret society—the Yorkish Rite to oppose the dominant Scottish Rite. . . .
>
> The Yorkish Rite, introduced by Poinsett, was the natural rallying point for those who had been disappointed in the shareout of benefits; it was made up of the lawless elements of the Revolution—the Villas and Zapatas of the revolution of 1910—and was republican, proletarian and fiercely irreligious in character. Five lodges were organized with local chiefs. . . . Soon the two Rites were divided not only by political views but by personal vendettas. For fifty years the history of Mexico becomes a series of coups and plots, assassinations and executions; of embezzlement and bribery; the learned and charitable institutions were sacked to provide funds for rival gangs; the work of three centuries of civilized rule was obliterated in a generation, leaving the nation bankrupt, discredited abroad and divided by irreconcilable hatred at home.[5]

[5] Evelyn Waugh, *Robbers under Law* (London: Chapman and Hall, 1939), pp. 126–28.

Mexican revolutionists Benito Juárez, Ignacio Ramírez, and Porfirio Díaz were all Freemasons, as were most of their close associates. Through their efforts, all Church property was confiscated, and even today no church or religious organization is permitted to own any property in Mexico whatsoever. Every church of whatever denomination, as well as every monastery and convent, is owned by the Mexican government, which permits congregations to use the premises for religious purposes. Technically, even the wearing of a clerical collar or religious habit violates Mexican law.

Elsewhere in Latin America, most of those who led the fight against Spain for the independence of their countries were Masons: Simón Bolívar of Venezuela, Bernardo O'Higgins of Chile, José Martí of Cuba, and others. Since the Catholic Church sided with Spain and the ruling powers, they were robustly anticlerical.

Today there are Grand Lodges or Grand Orients in Argentina, Bolivia, Costa Rica, Cuba, the Dominican Republic, Ecuador, Guatamala, Chile, Nicaragua, Panama, Paraguay, Peru, El Salvador, Uruguay, and Venezuela. Brazil counts twenty-three Grand Lodges, and Colombia six. Only one of the twenty-one Grand Lodges in Mexico is recognized by more than a handful of U.S. Grand Lodges.

A joint pastoral letter by the bishops of Argentina in 1959 reminded the faithful that the aims of Catholicism and Freemasonry "are contradictory and absolutely exclude each other". They added that secularism is the "ideological expression proper to Freemasonry".

The only other sizable bodies of Masons are those in Australia and New Zealand, where an estimated 365,000 men wear the square and compass, and in the Philippines.

Each U.S. Grand Lodge maintains a list of Grand Lodges and Grand Orients to which it gives official recognition. All

Grand Lodges in this country recognize the Grand Lodges of England, Scotland, Ireland, and Canada and the Grand Orient of Italy, but the pattern of recognition for other Grand Lodges can be bewildering. For example, the Grand Lodge of California recognizes the Grand Lodge of Bolivia, but Alabama does not; Indiana recognizes Uruguay, but neighboring Illinois does not. The Grand Lodge of Louisiana recognizes ninety-seven other Grand Lodges and Grand Orients, but Mississippi has only fifty-five on its approved list. Any U.S. Mason who visits a lodge of an unrecognized jurisdiction risks Masonic punishment, and visitors from such lodges may not be admitted to lodge meetings.

Masons and anti-Masons have often inflated the influence of the lodge in historical events such as the French Revolution. However, as the recent P2 conspiracy demonstrates, the potential for illegal activities under the protection of Masonic secrecy cannot be discounted.

CHAPTER XI

THE CHRISTIAN AND THE LODGE

Why Would a Christian Join the Lodge?

For hundreds of millions of Roman Catholics and Eastern Orthodox, and tens of millions of Protestants, the choice is clear. They may follow the admonition of their churches and avoid the lodge, or they may join the Masonic lodge and thereby reject the spiritual direction of their pope, bishops, or church leaders. If they follow the latter path, the churches recognize their divided allegiance by various penalties, ranging from a reprimand to denial of full participation in the church to expulsion.

We believe that anyone who has followed our discussion to this point will agree that this is the only course of action that a Christian church can pursue. The Masonic lodge may avoid anticlerical activities in certain nations, may support commendable charitable undertakings, may disclaim its own religious orientation. Nevertheless, the Christian knows that he cannot worship the Triune God on Sunday morning and the Great Architect on lodge night. He knows he cannot participate in religious worship with non-Christians praying to the G.A.O.T.U. and still observe Christ's command to ask the Father in his name.

Masonic friends may assure us that the lodge itself does not bar Catholics or other Christians from membership and that nothing detrimental to the Church has ever been voiced in their temples. This may very well be true, but it is quite beside the point. Christians do not feel free to become Buddhists simply because Buddhists may refrain from attacking Christianity. They do not become Buddhists or Muslims because Christ, not Buddha or Muhammed, is the Way, the Truth, and the Life.

For Masonry, the Bible is one of many acceptable Volumes of the Sacred Law but not the unique revelation of God to man. Jesus was a great religious teacher, but so were the founders of Islam and Buddhism and the other world religions. Belief in baptism and the other sacraments, the Trinity, grace, and the central doctrines of the Christian faith are irrelevant in the lodge. Masonry relegates these to the categories of "sectarian" and "peculiar" dogmas, and those who believe in them are warned not to drag them into the temples of Masonry's universal religion. Masonry carries man back to a pre-Christian reliance on human reason alone, with absolutely no reference to the Christian revelation. We readily admit that a belief in a supreme being and in the immortality of the soul is better than atheism. Masonry, however, does not labor to convert twentieth-century atheists and agnostics to theism; the lodge offers Christian men a pre-Christian religious worship, theology, and morality.

What possible advantages would a Christian see in the lodge that would induce him to seek admission into Masonry? We find a number of such advantages dangled before prospective members, but none of these withstands examination.

In the first place, the lodge promises to make its initiates privy to great secrets. They will be "in" while the rest of mankind, including most of Christendom, will sit in the darkness outside. Nowhere does Masonry promise more and deliver less; the great secrets of the lodge are neither great nor secret. Are these the secrets of the universe? Are these secrets too blinding in brilliance for the minds of women, children, and the "profane"? Are they the keys to spiritual, physical, and mental happiness? Alas, they consist of a few passwords and secret grips and ritual mumbo-jumbo. The dissatisfied Master Mason must be enticed by the carrot of higher and higher degrees to find the secrets he expected in the Blue Lodge. He never finds them.

What is more, the secrets are not even secret. He should have known that real secrets in a mass organization of 2,100,000 men are illusory. Anyone with curiosity about the subject can easily procure all the genuine Masonic rituals he wishes.

Other candidates for the lodge are attracted by the promise of preference. Once they become eligible to wear the Masonic ring or lapel button, certainly their business will pick up; they will sell more life insurance, or they will gain more patients or clients. Perhaps if they get into legal difficulties, they will find a brother Mason on the bench or in the jury box. And should they decide to run for public office, they will enjoy the electoral support of their brethren of the white apron.

A Mason may find some doors open to him that would otherwise have remained shut, and he may pick up a few votes that would have gone to the opposition candidate. He would be foolish to think, however, that more than a handful of Americans make it a practice to investigate lodge membership in their complex daily activities.

Not that possible preferential treatment of Masons by their brothers is unknown. In fact, secular critics of the lodge, such as Stephen Knight, have asked how well a democratic society can function if judges and jurors, detectives and policemen, tax collectors and personnel managers have sworn to give preferential treatment to fellow lodge members.[1]

We do not wish to deprecate the charitable activities of the Blue Lodge, another advantage that attracts some candidates, but we must say that there is no comparison between the charity of the Christian churches and that of the lodge. While the lodge carefully limits its disbursements to those who are paid-up Masons, the Church extends her charity to all. The regular lodges take pains to exclude women, children, blacks, the poor, and the physically handicapped from their temples. The men accepted for membership in the lodge are those who are least likely ever to need financial assistance. (No one wants to take credit away from the Shriners for the magnificent work they do in their twenty-two hospitals for children, but as every Mason and student of fraternalism knows, the Shrine is not a part of "pure and ancient Masonry" but simply a fun organization that enrolls Masons. In turn, we assume that most Masons acknowledge the contribution made by the nine hundred health-care facilities sponsored by Catholics, as well as the scores under Methodist, Lutheran, and other church auspices.)

Actually, anyone who expects to rely on the lodge for financial help in a serious situation, such as long-term unemployment or a major medical problem, would be better advised to put his contribution into insurance, certificates of deposit, annuities, common stocks, or bonds. The nominal amounts collected from lodge members can hardly stretch to meet the serious financial needs of more than one or two members.

[1] Stephen Knight, *The Brotherhood: The Secret World of Freemasons* (New York: Stein and Day, 1984).

Good fellowship is another promise the lodge makes its candidates, and we will not deny that such fellowship flourishes in many lodges. It should. Practically all the members fall into the same social class: white, middle-class, Protestant. Such jarring topics as religion and politics are outlawed. "Nonconformists" may be excluded by means of the blackball. Again, what a difference between the exclusive lodge and the all-embracing Church of Christ, which turns no one from her doors.

Except in the smallest towns, the opportunities for making business contacts and enjoying fellowship are so abundant that no one need feel he is sacrificing much by following the advice of his church and shunning the lodge. A Roman Catholic, for example, can join the Kiwanis, Lions, Elks, Eagles, Chamber of Commerce, Jaycees, Moose, Knights of Columbus, American Legion, a political party, Serra Club, Veterans of Foreign Wars, Exchange, Rotary, and dozens of other civic and service organizations.

Finally, some men are wooed into the lodge by simple vanity, by the opportunity to claim grandiose titles, to command a respect that they do not find in their own homes or in their occupations. Some find an escape from an oppressively feminine social life in the all-male lodge. In his popular sociological study *The Status Seekers*, Vance Packard observed:

> The fraternal orders reached their peak of popularity in the 1920's, when most of the adult males of America belonged to one or more. Their secrecy and rituals and costumes may seem a bit juvenile today, but these orders did make one important contribution to democracy. Like the Roman Catholic Church, they embraced the span of the American social order. The lodge hall was an excellent place for people of all classes to become acquainted, and

to understand each other's problems and aspirations. Such an opportunity to make oneself known to people of the superior class is an essential precondition to winning acceptance into their class, in case one has ambitions. The fraternal orders performed, at least, that vital function of providing a common ground for intermingling. A generation ago in Jonesville, W. Lloyd Warner points out, "every important man in the community was a Mason, and often an Odd Fellow or a Woodman." And the man who managed to become a high-degree Mason was taking a long, sure stride toward social success. Today, the situation has changed abruptly not only in Jonesville but throughout America. The members of the two upper classes have abandoned the lodges almost completely in favor of their exclusive civic-type groups; and typically, the lower classes have not been able to follow them into these.[2]

In recent years Freemasonry has lost its attraction for young college graduates. Of course, some young men might petition for membership because of a family tradition; their fathers and grandfathers may have been Masons. The pool of possible candidates has been shrinking as Roman Catholics, Lutherans, Mormons, and conservative and "born-again" Christians have entered the middle and upper middle classes, the traditional hunting ground for new members. For these and other reasons the Masonic lodges have been losing substantial numbers of members since 1959.

Masonry may be in a decline, but many fine men still value their lodge membership. No one wants to stir up antagonism between the lodge and the churches. Dialogue between Christians and Masons can lessen hostility between these groups. Cooperation in civic and charitable works can

[2] Vance Packard, *The Status Seekers* (New York: David McKay Co., 1959), pp. 192–93.

be encouraged. Some Christians believe the most fantastic things about Masonry and should be helped to form a more rational judgment. Some Masons see the Church, especially the Roman Catholic Church, as the Church of the Inquisition or the Crusades and the prop for discredited monarchies. No one benefits from such caricatures.

When all is said and done, secret societies such as Masonry have little to offer the Christian churches in their search for greater unity. False ecumenism, which ignores the basic differences between Masonic naturalism and Christianity, or the desire of a few men to find in the lodge a fellowship, a better chance for promotion, or a few more customers than they can find through other community organizations, is no reason to minimize the serious objections to Freemasonry raised by the churches.

Christians must respect the decision of others to affiliate with the lodge, but more and more Christians have come to realize that the Great Architect of the Universe is not the God Jesus taught them to call Our Father.

APPENDIX

*Declaration of the Sacred Congregation
for the Doctrine of the Faith, 1983*

The question has been raised whether the Church's position on Masonic associations has been altered, especially since no explicit mention is made of them in the new Code of Canon Law, as there was in the old code.

This sacred congregation is able to reply that circumstance is to be attributed to a criterion adopted in drafting. This criterion was observed also in regard to other associations which were likewise passed over in silence, because they were included in broader categories.

The Church's negative position on Masonic associations therefore remains unaltered, since their principles have always been regarded as irreconcilable with the Church's doctrine. Hence joining them remains prohibited by the Church. Catholics enrolled in Masonic associations are involved in serious sin and may not approach Holy Communion.

Local Ecclesiastical authorities do not have the faculty to pronounce a judgment on the nature of Masonic associations which might include a diminution of the above-mentioned judgment, in accordance with the intention of this congregation's declaration delivered on February 17, 1981 (cf. AAS 73 [1981], pp. 240–241).

The Supreme Pontiff John Paul II approved this declaration, deliberated at an ordinary meeting of this sacred congregation, and ordered it to become part of public law.

Rome. From the office of the Sacred Congregation for the Doctrine of the Faith, November 26, 1983.

> Joseph Cardinal Ratzinger,
> *Prefect*
>
> Jerome Hamer, O.P.,
> *Titular Archbishop of Loria, Secretary*

GLOSSARY

Acacia A type of thorny flowering tree or shrub that grows in warm climates. In the Hiramic legend, a sprig of acacia was placed at the head of Hiram Abiff's grave and came to symbolize immortality. Masons throw sprigs of acacia or evergreens on the coffin of a deceased brother.

Anno Lucis Latin for "In the year of Light". In Masonic documents the dates are given *Anno Lucis* rather than *Anno Domini* ("In the year of the Lord"). The world was once thought to have been created four thousand years before the birth of Christ; with creation came light. Masons add four thousand years to the Anno Domini date. Thus 1998 would become 5998.

Blue Lodges Lodges in which the first three degrees are conferred. Also known as Symbolic lodges. They make up the basic unit of the Masonic system and are called Blue because this is the official color of Freemasonry.

Clandestine A lodge that is not legally constituted. In the eyes of white regular Masonry, the predominantly black Prince Hall lodges are clandestine.

Cowan An eavesdropper on Masonic rites, or someone who pretends to be a Mason but has not undergone the proper initiations.

Craft Knowledge and practice of speculative Freemasonry in the Blue Lodges; person holding such knowledge; term for secrets adapted to simulate the working skills of medieval stonemasons.

Demit Permission given a Mason to terminate his membership. It must be granted to anyone who asks for it who is in good standing and about whom no charges have been or are about to be preferred.

Doctrine of the Perfect Youth About half of the U.S. Grand Lodges refuse to initiate anyone with a serious physical disability. This regulation dates to the fourth of the Old Charges, which states: "No Master should take an Apprentice, unless he has sufficient Employment for him, and unless he be a perfect Youth, having no Maim or Defect in his Body. . . ."

Due Guard Movements of the arm and hands that identify a particular degree. Each of the three basic degrees has its own due guard.

Entered Apprentice First degree of Blue Lodge Freemasonry.

Fellow Craft Second degree of Blue Lodge Freemasonry.

Five Points of Fellowship Posture assumed in the Master Mason's degree: foot to foot, knee to knee, breast to breast, hand to back, and cheek to cheek or mouth to ear.

G.A.O.T.U. The Great (or Grand) Architect of the Universe. The god of Masonry.

Grand Orient A Masonic jurisdiction in Europe or Latin America that corresponds to a Grand Lodge in Anglo-Saxon Masonry.

Grips Various types of handshakes by which Masons recognize one another and the degrees they have attained. Also called tokens.

Landmarks Fundamental beliefs and practices of Freemasonry that cannot be changed by any Grand Lodge, such as the Legend of the third degree and the observance of secrecy in the lodge. Masons do not agree on the number of such landmarks.

Ma-hah-bone The Grand Masonic Word of the Master Mason's degree, which is given on the five points of fellowship.

Master The head of a Blue Lodge. The only proper form of address is Worshipful Master.

Master Mason Third and highest degree of Blue Lodge Freemasonry.

Profane Someone who has not been initiated into the inner mysteries, i.e., a non-Mason.

Sign Gestures to indicate the death penalty a Mason is under in a particular degree.

"So Mote It Be" The Masonic conclusion to prayers to the G.A.O.T.U., which corresponds to the Christian "Amen."

Speculative Freemasonry The use of stonemasons' tools and terminology to impart philosophical and religious knowledge. Operative Masonry enrolled craftsmen who actually cut and placed stones and built cathedrals, palaces, and public buildings.

Tyler The guard outside the lodge-room door. He must ascertain if those seeking entry are Masons in good standing.

V.S.L. The Volume of the Sacred Law. Any book that symbolizes religious beliefs: the Bible, the Koran, the Vedas, the Bhagavad–Gita, etc. Where most of the lodge members are Christians, the V.S.L. will be the Old and New Testaments and will be placed on the altar in the Masonic temple.

BIBLIOGRAPHY

Acker, J. W. *Strange Altars: A Scriptural Appraisal of the Lodge.* St. Louis: Concordia, 1959.

The Ancient Arabic Order of the Nobles of the Mystic Shrine. Chicago: Ezra A. Cook, 1921.

Ankerberg, John. *The Secret Teachings of the Masonic Lodge.* Chicago: Moody Press, 1990.

Beha, Ernest. *A Comprehensive Dictionary of Freemasonry.* New York: Citadel Press, 1963.

Blanchard, Charles A. *Modern Secret Societies.* Chicago: National Christian Association, 1938.

Box, Hubert S. *The Nature of Freemasonry.* London: Augustine Press, 1952.

Cahill, E. *Freemasonry and the Anti-Christian Movement.* Dublin, N.H.: Gill & Son, 1952.

Campbell-Everden, William Preston. *Freemasonry and Its Etiquette.* New York: Weathervane, 1978.

Cerza, Alphonse. *Anti-Masonry.* Fulton, Mo.: Missouri Lodge of Research, 1962.

———. *"Let There Be Light": A Study in Anti-Masonry.* Silver Spring, Md.: Masonic Service Association, 1977.

Chase, George Wingate. *Digest of Masonic Law,* 3d ed. New York: Macoy and Sickles, 1864.

Coil, Henry Wilson. *Coil's Masonic Encyclopedia.* New York: Macoy, 1961.

Darrah, Delmar Duane. *History and Evolution of Freemasonry.* Chicago: Charles T. Powner, 1951.

De Poncins, Vicomte Leon. *Freemasonry and the Vatican: A Struggle for Recognition*. London: Britons, 1968.

Dillon, George E. *Freemasonry Unmasked*. London: Britons, 1959.

Dumenil, Lynn. *Freemasonry and American Culture*. Princeton, N.J.: Princeton University Press, 1984.

Duncan, Malcolm C. *Duncan's Masonic Ritual and Monitor*. Chicago: Ezra A. Cook, 1952.

Fahey, Denis. *The Kingship of Christ and Organized Naturalism*. Dublin: Holy Ghost Missionary College, 1949.

Ferguson, Charles W. *Fifty Million Brothers*. New York: Farrar and Rinehart, 1937.

Finney, Charles G. *Character and Claims of Freemasonry*. Chicago: National Christian Association, 1948.

Fisher, Paul A. *Behind the Lodge Door*. Washington, D.C.: Shield, 1988.

Goodwin, S. J. *Mormonism and Masonry*. Washington, D.C.: Masonic Service Association, 1924.

Graebner, Theodore. *A Handbook of Organizations*. St. Louis: Concordia, 1948.

———. *Is Masonry a Religion?* St. Louis: Concordia, 1946.

Hannah, Walton. *Darkness Visible*. London: Augustine Press, 1952.

———. *Christian by Degrees*. London: Augustine Press, 1954.

Harris, Jack. *Freemasonry: The Invisible Cult in Our Midst*. Towson, Md.: Jack Harris, 1983.

Haywood, H. L. *Freemasonry and Roman Catholicism*. Chicago: Masonic History Co., 1943.

———. *The Great Teachings of Masonry*. New York: George H. Doran, 1923.

Haywood, H. L., and James E. Craig. *A History of Freemasonry*. New York: John Day, 1927.

Holly, James L. *The Southern Baptist Convention and Freemasonry*. Beaumont, Tex.: Mission and Ministry to Men, 1993.

Johnston, Humphrey J. T. *Freemasonry: A Short Historical Sketch.* London: Catholic Truth Society, 1952.

Jones, Bernard E. *Freemason's Guide and Compendium.* London: George G. Harrap, 1950.

Kelly, Clarence. *Conspiracy against God and Man.* Belmont, Mass.: Western Islands, 1974.

Knight, Stephen. *The Brotherhood: The Secret World of the Freemasons.* New York: Stein and Day, 1984.

Lepper, J. Herron. *Famous Secret Societies.* London: Sampson, Low, Marston & Co., 1938.

Macdonald, Fergus. *The Catholic Church and the Secret Societies in the United States.* New York: United States Catholic Historical Society, 1946.

MacKenzie, Norman, ed. *Secret Societies.* New York: Holt, Rinehart & Winston, 1967.

Mackey, Albert G. *Lexicon of Freemasonry.* New York: Maynard, Merrill & Co., 1871.

———. *Masonic Ritualist.* New York: Clark & Maynard, 1869.

———. *Symbolism of Freemasonry.* Revised by Robert I. Clegg. Chicago: Masonic History Co., 1946.

———. *Encyclopedia of Freemasonry.* Philadelphia: L. H. Everts, 1887.

———. *A Text Book of Masonic Jurisprudence.* New York: Maynard, Merrill & Co., 1859.

Macoy, Robert. *Masonic Burial Services with General Instructions.* Chicago: Ezra A. Cook, 1954.

McGavin, E. Cecil. *Mormonism and Masonry.* Salt Lake City: Bookcraft, 1956.

McReavy, Lawrence L. *Forbidden and Suspect Societies.* London: Catholic Truth Society, 1956.

Mellor, Alec. *Our Separated Brethren: The Freemasons.* London: George G. Harrap, 1964.

Morey, Robert. *The Truth about Masons*. Eugene, Ore.: Harvest House, 1993.

Morgan, William. *Freemasonry Exposed*. Batavia, N.Y., 1827.

Newton, Joseph Fort. *The Builders*. Cedar Rapids, Iowa: The Torch Press, 1915.

Nickel, Theodore F., and James G. Manz. *A Christian View of Freemasonry*. St. Louis: Concordia, 1957.

Pick, Fred L., and G. Norman Knight. *The Pocket History of Freemasonry*. New York: Philosophical Library, 1953.

Pike, Albert. *Morals and Dogma*. Charleston, S.C.: Supreme Council of the Thirty-third Degree for the Southern Jurisdiction of the United States, 1881.

Preuss, Arthur. *A Dictionary of Secret and Other Societies*. St. Louis: B. Herder Book Co., 1924.

——. *A Study in American Freemasonry*, 2d ed. St. Louis: B. Herder Book Co., 1908.

Quigley, Joseph A. M. *Condemned Societies*. Washington, D.C.: Catholic University of America Press, 1927.

Revised Knight Templarism. Chicago: Ezra A. Cook, 1944.

Rice, John R. *Lodges Examined by the Bible*. Wheaton, Ill.: Sword of the Lord Publishers, 1943.

Roberts, Allen E. *Freemasonry in American History*. Richmond, Va.: Macoy, 1985.

——. *Masonic Trivia and Facts*. Highland Springs, Va.: Anchor Communications, 1994.

Robinson, John J. *Born in Blood: The Lost Secret of Freemasonry*. New York: M. Evans, 1989.

Ronayne, Edmond. *The Master's Carpet*. Chicago: Ezra A. Cook, 1879.

——. *Ronayne's Handbook of Freemasonry*. Chicago: Ezra A. Cook, 1955.

Rosen, Peter. *The Catholic Church and Secret Societies*. Milwaukee: Houkamp & Cannon, 1902.

Scotch Rite Masonry Illustrated. Chicago: Ezra A. Cook, 1953, 2 vols.

Shaw, James, and Tom C. McKenney. *The Deadly Deception*. Lafayette, La.: Huntington House, 1988.

Stevens, Albert C. *The Cyclopaedia of Fraternities*. New York: E. B. Treat and Co., 1907.

Stillson, Henry Leonard. *History of the Ancient and Honorable Fraternity of Free and Accepted Masons and Concordant Orders*. Boston: Fraternity Publishing Co., 1912.

Tanner, Jerald, and Sandra Tanner. *Mormonism, Magic and Masonry*. Salt Lake City: Utah Lighthouse Ministry, 1983.

Van Cott, Charles. *Freemasonry: A Sleeping Giant*. Minneapolis: T. S. Denison & Co., 1959.

Van Deventer, Fred. *Parade to Glory: The Story of the Shriners and Their Hospitals for Crippled Children*. New York: William Morrow, 1959.

"Vindex". *Light Invisible, the Freemason's Answer to Darkness Visible*. London: Regency Press, 1952.

Voorhis, Harold V. B. *Masonic Organizations and Allied Orders and Degrees*. Red Bank, N.J.: Henry Emmerson, 1952.

Walkes, Joseph A., Jr. *Black Square & Compass: 200 Years of Prince Hall Freemasonry*. Richmond, Va.: Macoy, 1979.

Ward, J. S. M. *The Masonic Why and Wherefore*. London: Baskerville Press, 1929.

Webster, Nesta H. *Secret Societies and Subversive Movements*. London: Britons, 1955.

Whalen, William J. *Handbook of Secret Organizations*. Milwaukee: Bruce, 1966.

Williams, Loretta J. *Black Freemasonry and Middle-Class Realities*. Columbia, Mo.: University of Missouri Press, 1980.

Williamson, Harry A. *The Prince Hall Primer*. Chicago: Ezra A. Cook, 1957.

INDEX

Acacia fraternity, 134
Acacian, definition of, 112, 197
Adair, Forrest, 125
Adams, John Quincy, on
    Masonry, 17
Adoptive Masonry, 133
Affaire des fiches, 174–75
Allegory, Masonic, 15
Altar, Masonic, 109
Amaranth, Order of, 133
American Rite. *See* York Rite
Amish churches, 157
Ancient and Accepted Rite, 81;
    English, 84
Ancient Arabic Order Nobles of
    the Mystic Shrine. *See* Shrine
Ancient Egyptian Arabic Order
    Nobles of the Mystic Shrine,
    135
Anderson, James, 37
Anglican Church, 160–61
Ankerberg, John, 155
Anno Lucis, 197
Anti-Catholicism, 24–27, 88, 93
Anti-Masonic Party, 20
Antients, 38, 43
Apron, Masonic, 52
Argentinian bishops, on Masonry,
    185

Arnold, Benedict, 19
Assemblies of God, 153
Ataturk, Kemal, 182
Attendance requirements, 13, 31
Australia, Masonry in, 185

Ballot, Masonic, 41–42
Baptist Bible Fellowship, 160
Baptist Churches, 159–60
Belgium, Masonry in, 176
Benedict XIV, 138, 141
Benedict XV, 143
Bible, 49, 109–10. *See also* Volume of the Sacred Law
Black, Hugo 23
Black Masons, 13, 16. *See also* Prince Hall Lodges
Blakemore, Louis, 80
Blanchard, Charles A., 161
Blue lodges, 28, 79, 197
Boaz, 52
Bolsheviks, 182–83
Bonaparte, Joseph, 173, 177
Book of Constitutions, 37
Booth, General William, 162
"Born-again" Christians, 156
Box, Hubert S., 7, 160
British Methodist Church, 158–59

O'Connell, Daniel, 137
Oaths: Entered Apprentice, 49–
    50; Fellow Craft, 57–58;
    Knight Kadosh, 88–93;
    Masonic, 115–20; Master
    Mason, 62–65; Shrine, 116,
    129–30
Odd Fellows, 21
OES. *See* Eastern Star
Officers, lodge, 42
Oliver, George, 34
Order of Amaranth, 133
Order of Builders, 133
Order of Rainbow for Girls, 134
Order of the Golden Key, 134
Organizations, allied Masonic,
    121–35
Orthodox Presbyterian Church,
    165

P2 Lodge, 178–81
Packard, Vance, 191–92
Papal condemnations of Masonry,
    136–49
Paul VI, 181
Peale, Norman Vincent, 167
Penalty, ecclesiastical, 13, 136,
    143, 145, 195
Pentecostal Churches, 153
Pentecostal Holiness Church, 153
Petition for Masonic initiation,
    41–42
Philaletes Society, 134
Philalethes, The, 134, 155
Pick, Fred L., 35
Pike, Albert, authority on Ma-
    sonry, 8; and the Ku Klux
    Klan, 21; Leo Taxil on, 140;
    on name of God, 94; patriarch

of Scottish rite, 8, 81–83; and
    Prince Hall lodge, 29; on Prot-
    estantism, 155–52; racism of,
    21, 29; on religion and Ma-
    sonry, 102, 107–8,
    110; on unity of Masonry,
    142–43
Pius IX, Pope, 138–39, 141
Poinsett, Joel, 184
Portugal, Masonry in, 177–78
Presbyterian Church in America,
    165
Presidents of U.S., Masonic, 16–
    17
Preuss, Arthur, 7
Prince Hall lodges, 13, 16, 29, 30,
    135
Profanes, 8, 41, 199
Propaganda Due lodge, 178–81
Protestantism and Masonry, 16,
    21, 150–68

Quakers, 157

Racism, Masonic, 28–29
Rainbow Girls, 134
Ramsey, Chevalier, 80
Randel, William Pierce, 22
Ratzinger, Joseph Cardinal, 147
Reformed Presbyterian Church,
    165
Religion, Masonic, 37–38, 100–
    114
Representatives in Congress, Ma-
    sonic, 17
Reynolds, John B., 24
Rite of Memphis, 80
Rite of Perfection, 81
Ritual, Masonic, 40–77

Separated Brethren

Christian Family Finance

Catholics on Campus

Armageddon around the Corner: A Report on Jehovah's Witnesses

Faiths for the Few

The Latter-Day Saints in the Modern-Day World

Handbook of Secret Organizations

Minority Religions in America

Effective Publications for Colleges and Universities (with Kelvin J. Arden)

Other Religions in a World of Change (with Carl J. Pfeifer)

How Different Christian Churches Celebrate the Sacraments

Strange Gods: Contemporary Religious Cults in America

The Search for Common Ground (with James Davidson et al.)